The Comp[lete]

Keto For Two

Beginners Cookbook

More than 300 Ketogenic Recipes for Couples with 3 Weeks Meal Plan for Effective Weight Loss.

By Clarion Ulreich

The Complete
Keto For Two Beginners Cookbook

All Rights Reserved. No part of this publication may be reproduced in any form or by any means, including scanning, photocopying, or otherwise without prior written permission of the copyright holder. Copyright © 2019

The Complete
Keto For Two Beginners Cookbook

Table o02f Contents

DEDICATION 3

TABLE OF CONTENTS 4

INTRODUCTION 15

CHAPTER ONE: INTRODUCTION TO THE KETO DIET 16

What is the Ketogenic Diet? 16

How to Lose Weight with the Ketogenic Diet? 17

Keto Friendly Foods 20

Foods to Avoid On Keto Diet 24

Keto Pantry Essential 26

Keto Friendly Alternatives 27

Testing for Ketosis 29

FAQS About Keto Diet 29

Keto for Diabetics 32

Exercising in Keto 35

CHAPTER TWO: 21-DAY MEAL PLAN 36

Day 1 36

Day 2 36

DAY 3 36

Day 4 37

Clarion Ulreich

Dedication

This book is dedicated to all couples who wants to keep fit

Day 5 37

Day 6 37
    Day 7 37
    Day 8 38
    Day 9 38

Day 10 38

Day 11 38

Day 12 39

Day 13 39

Day 14 40

Day 15 40

Day 16 40

Day 17 40

Day 18 41

Day 19 41

Day 20 41

Day 21 41

CHAPTER THREE: SNACKS & DESSERTS 43

Zucchini Parmesan Chips 43

Skinny Cocktail Meatballs 44

White Chocolate Butter Pecan Fat Bombs 46

Keto Lava Cake 48

Low Carb Paleo Almond Flour Pie Crust 49

Keto Strawberry Mini Clafoutis 51

Keto Chocolate Dairy Free Ice Cream 53

No Bake Peanut Butter Protein Bars 54

Keto Chocolate Dairy Free Ice Cream 55

Jalapeno Turkey Tomato Bites 56

Bell Pepper Boats 57

Party Spiced Cheese Chips 58

Hard-Boiled Eggs Stuffed with Ricotta Cheese 59

Asparagus & Chorizo Traybake 60

Keto Pie Crust 61

Speedy Italian Appetizer Balls 63

Quail Eggs & Prosciutto 64

Tomato & Cheese in Lettuce Packets 65

Zucchini & Avocado Eggs with Pork Sausage 66

Crab Salad Stuffed Avocado 67

CHAPTER THREE: BREAKFAST & SMOOTHIES RECIPES 69

Scotch Eggs 69

Rolled Smoked Salmon with Salmon & Cheese 71

Breadless Breakfast Sandwich 72

Poultry Patties 74

Broccoli, Egg & Pancetta Gratin 75

Spinach Nests with Egg and Cheese 77

Avocado Shake	78
Pesto Mug Sandwiches with Bacon & Ricotta	79
Quesadillas with Bacon & Mushrooms	81
Ham & Cheese Keto Sandwiches	83
Chili Avocado Boats	84
Breakfast Serrano Ham Frittata with Fresh Salad	85
Microwave Bacon Mug Eggs	87
Peanut Butter & Pastrami Gofres	88
Lettuce Wraps	89
Breakfast Blueberry Coconut Smoothie	90
Chorizo Sausage Egg Cakes	91
Morning Herbed Eggs	92
Power Green Smoothie	94
Spinach Blueberry Smoothie	95
Peanut Butter Cup Smoothie	96
Lemon Cashew Smoothie	97
Yummy Blue Cheese & Mushroom Omelet	98
Roasted Stuffed Avocados	99
Asparagus & Goat Cheese Frittata	100
Golden Turmeric Latte with Nutmeg	102
Strawberry Chia Seed Pudding in Glass Jars	103
Sausage Cakes with Poached Eggs	104

Lettuce Cups Filled Mushrooms & Cheese 105

CHAPTER FIVE: POULTRY RECIPES 106

Keto Chicken Tenders 106

Paleo garlic chicken nuggets recipe 108

Asian chicken wraps with tahini tamari sauce 110

Chicken Thighs with Pan Gravy 111

Protein Pancakes 113

Jalapeno Popper Scrambled Eggs 114

Teriyaki Turkey Bowls 115

Breakfast Pizza 117

Chicken Nuggets 118

Mighty Meaty Pizza 119

Bacon Cheddar Omelette 120

Spinach Onion Goat Cheese Omelette 121

Low Carb Buffalo Chicken Meatballs 122

Chicken Wings with Lemons & Capers 123

Creamy Chicken with Pancetta, Mushrooms & Spinach 125

Creamy Mushroom & White Wine Chicken 127

Mediterranean Chicken 129

Chicken Wings with Lemon Jalapeno Peppers 131

Cheese and Bacon Stuffed Chicken 133

Grilled Turkey Drumsticks 135

Chicken Salad 137

Italian Chicken Meatballs 139

Eggplant & Carrot Chicken Gratin 141

Greek-Style Chicken Melange 143

Sunday Chicken Bake 145

Feta & Bacon Chicken 147

Baked Cheese Chicken Tenders 149

Sauced Chicken Legs with Vegetables 150

Rosemary Chicken with Avocado Sauce 152

Sage Chicken with Kale & Mushrooms 154

Paprika Chicken 156

Carrot & Mushroom Chicken Skillet 158

Cabbage & Broccoli Chicken Casserole 160

Lemon Butter Chicken 162

CHAPTER SIX: SEA FOODS 164

Fish Jambalaya 164

Greek Sea Bass with Olive Sauce 166

Sardines with Green Pasta & Sun-Dried Tomatoes 167

Saucy Cod with Mustard Greens 168

Baked Cod with Parmesan & Almonds 170

Fish Tacos with Slaw, Lemon and Cilantro 171

Fried Oysters in The Oven 173

Tuna with Greens and Blueberries (One Pot) 174

Roasted Old Bay Prawns 176

Three-Minute Lobster Tail 178

Crispy Salmon with Broccoli & Red Bell Pepper 180

Easy Baked Halibut Steaks 182

Mediterranean Tilapia Bake 184

Omelet Wraps with Tuna 186

Baked Trout and Asparagus Foil Packets 187

Coconut Shrimp 189

Bacon-Wrapped Scallop Cups (One Pot) 190

Sea Bass with Vegetables and Dill Sauce 192

Grilled Tuna Steaks with Shirataki Pad Thai 194

Country Club Crab Cakes 196

Coconut Fried Shrimp with Cilantro Sauce 197

Shrimp Sti-fry 199

Baked Salmon with Lemon and Mush 200

Pan-fried Soft Shell Crab 202

Chilli Cod with Chive Sauce 203

Pan-Seared Scallops with Sausage & Mozzarella 205

CHAPTER SEVEN: BEEF & PORK RECIPES 207

Secret Seasoning Sirloin Steak 207

Slopy Joes 208

Fajita Kabobs	209
Mini Meatloaves with Spinach	211
Cabbage Slaw with Ground Beef (One Pot)	213
Sticky Barbecued Ribs	214
Kielbasa and Sauerkraut (One Pot)	216
Rich and Easy Pork Ragout	217
Mexican Style Beef Casserole	219
Pork Loin Steaks in Creamy Pepper Sauce	221
Pork Medallions with Cabbage	223
Sticky Barbecued Ribs	225
Mom's Festive Meatloaf	227
Rich Winter Beef Stew	229
Beef and Garden Vegetable Soup	231
Chunky Pork Soup with Mustard Greens	233
Asian Spiced Beef with Broccoli	235
Easy Spicy Meatballs	237
Easy Spicy Meatballs	239
Veggie Beef Stew with Root Mash	241
Pulled Pork with Mint and Cheese	243
Roast Beef with Herbs	245
Pork Cutlets with Spanish Onion	246
Flank Steak Roll	247

Grilled Steak with Herb Butter & Green Beans 248

Beef Burgers with Iceberg Lettuce & Avocado 249

Juicy Beef with Rosemary & Thyme 251

Veggie Chuck Roast Beef in Oven 253

CHAPTER EIGHT: SOUPS, STEWS & SALADS 255

Chicken and Lime Soup 255

Fennel Salad 257

Spicy Habanero Cheeseburger Soup 258

Green Chicken Enchilada Soup 260

Cream" of Broccoli Soup 261

Creamy Zucchini Soup 262

Easy Pumpkin Soup 263

Spinach Salad with Goat Cheese & Pine Nuts 264

Pesto Caprese Salad with Tuna 265

Spinach Salad with Bacon & Mustard Vinaigrette 266

Caesar Salad 268

Keto Egg Salad 269

Classic Greek Salad 271

Salad of Prawns and Mixed Lettuce Greens 272

Pump up your Greens 'Creamed' Soup 273

Green Chicken Enchilada Soup 274

Spicy Habanero Cheeseburger Soup 275

Cream of Mushroom Soup 277

Minty Green Chicken Salad 279

Celery & Cauliflower Soup with Bacon Croutons 281

Avocado cucumber ginger salad recipe 283

Shrimp and Arugula Salad 284

Keto cucumber salad 285

Feta & Sun-Dried Tomato Salad with Bacon 286

Chinese Tofu Soup 287

CHAPTER TEN: VEGAN AND VEGETARIAN RECIPES 288

Almond Pancakes 288

Grilled Cauliflower Steaks with Haricots Vert 290

Scrambled Tofu 292

Easy Zoodles with Sauce and Parmesan 293

Keto Tortilla Wraps with Vegetables 294

Avocado-Mint Smoothie 296

Fruit Salad with Yogurt-Basil Dressing 297

Mediterranean Eggplant Squash Pasta 298

Bell Pepper Omelet 300

Apple-Walnut Granola 301

Broccoli Slaw with Tahini Dressing 302

Scrambled Egg with Feta 304

Roasted Cauliflower Gratin 305

The Complete
Keto For Two Beginners Cookbook

Easy Creamy Broccoli Soup 307

Mediterranean Cauliflower Quiche with Cheese 309

Chili & Blue Cheese Stuffed Mushrooms 311

Zucchini and Mushroom Lasagna 312

Burritos Wraps with Avocado & Cauliflower 314

Parmesan Fried Eggs 316

Red Beet Salad 317

Hot Pizza with Tomatoes, Cheese & Olives 319

Grilled Tofu Kabobs with Arugula Salad 321

Cream of Tomato Soup 323

Green Omelet 325

Zucchini Pasta with Caper Pesto 327

Zucchini Carpaccio 329

Scalloped Fennel 330

Pizza Bianca with Mushrooms 331

Introduction

If you've been in this weight loss struggle, by now you must have certainly heard about the Ketogenic diet and the many people who have had success losing weight and keeping fit through this diet plan.

The Ketogenic diet is known for losing weight through a strange phenomenon. It is called strange because for some people depending upon fats for losing fats sounds astonishing! We cannot normally imagine that we have to eat the same thing that we want to eliminate from our body - fats! The Ketogenic diet consists of high amounts of fats, ample proteins and fewer carbohydrates.

Not only can the keto diet promote weight loss, it also comes with numerous health benefits such as: Management of diabetes, lower cholesterol, improved mental clarity, lowers the risk of some cancers and lowers the risk of cardiovascular disease.

The keto diet requires that you change your eating habits. It's easier to make these adjustments when you have the participation and support of your partner or other family members. As a couple, you'll be able to encourage each other on those days that are more difficult than others for sticking to your food plan.

This book contains all you need to know about the Ketogenic diet as a beginner or a Pro. It is designed to be suitable for couples on the Ketogenic diet and consists of over 300 Keto recipes for couples with 21-day meal plan.

Chapter One: Introduction to the Keto Diet

What is the Ketogenic Diet?

You might have heard your friends talking about ketosis, the Ketogenic diet, etc. And, here you are researching about what they are talking about so passionately.

The Ketogenic diet has now become well known for losing weight through a strange phenomenon. It is called strange because for some people depending upon fats for losing fats sounds astonishing! We cannot normally imagine that we have to eat the same thing that we want to eliminate from our body - fats! The Ketogenic diet consists of high amounts of fats, ample proteins and fewer carbohydrates. It forces the body to use fats instead of carbs for breaking down to convert them into energy. In our regular diets, we consume more carbohydrate and shun fats. Thus, our body is perfectly adapted throughout history to break down carbohydrates for energy. However, in the Ketogenic diet, we try to change the pattern of our body to break down the elements to be used for energy. We feed our body with more fats and less carbohydrates and thus force it to adapt in a new way to use fats for energy.

The plus side to this diet is that you do not have to count your calories or the amount of fats you are consuming like the way you do in other diets. You can indulge in different types of meats and oils, do not feel guilty and still lose weight.

Normally, our body would convert food into glucose that would be transported to various body parts. This glucose is especially important in fueling functions of the brain. It is easiest for your body to convert carbs into glucose and use it as energy. Thus, it is obvious that your body will choose carbs over any other source of energy. Our body produces insulin to process glucose in the bloodstream and makes it travel around the body. Since glucose is there to provide energy to your body, fats are not required and hence, stored.

However, if you do not feed your body with carbohydrates, the liver starts converting fats to ketone bodies and fatty acids. These ketone bodies enter the brain and pass through it to replace the old source of energy, which was glucose. Thus, all the fats you consume in the form of meats, oils, creams, etc. is broken down and it does not get accumulated in your body.

When you lower down the carbs intake, the body is persuaded to enter into a state of ketosis. It is just a natural process, which is initiated by the body to help it survive when the food consumption is low. The Ketogenic diet is known by some other names as well- low carbs high fat diet (LCHF), low carb diet. The ultimate aim of a well maintained Ketogenic diet is to persuade the body into a metabolic state. But, this does not mean that you have to go hungry on calories. However, you just have to strictly control your consumption of carbohydrates. It is definitely easier than starving on fats. Human body is extremely adaptive to everything it is forced into. If you make it depend on a new source of energy rather than the regular one, it will adapt accordingly in a few days.

How to Lose Weight with the Ketogenic Diet?

The following tips should be applied while losing weight through the ketogenic diet plan:

1. **Choose a diet containing fewer carbohydrates**

You need to cut down on your consumption of starch and sugar. This idea is more than a century old. There have been a lot of diet plans which are based on reducing the amount of carbs you take. The new thing with the Ketogenic diet is that you provide your body with an alternate source of energy to depend on, which is fats. When you do not eat carbohydrates or eat them moderately, your body is capable of burning 300 additional calories per day, even when you are resting! It means that this amount of burnt calories is equal to a gym session of moderate physical activity.

2. Eat when you feel hungry

You do not need to stay hungry all the time to lose weight. This is the most common mistake committed by people who start a low carb diet. In the Ketogenic diet, you do not have to be scared of fats. Carbohydrates and fats are two major sources of energy for our body. If you are snatching carbs from your body, you need to give it an ample supply of fats. Low fats and low carbs equal to starvation, and we do not want that, do we? Starvation results in cravings and fatigue. That is why, people who starve give up easily on their diet plans. The better solution is to consume natural fat till the time you are satisfied. Some of the natural fats are full fat cream, butter, olive oil, meat, bacon, fatty fish, coconut oil, eggs.

3. Eat real food

This is one more common mistake made by Ketogenic followers that they get fooled by the fraudulent but creative marketing of "low-carb" foods. A real Ketogenic diet should be supported by real food. It implies the food which is being eaten by humans for millions of years. For example, fish, meat, vegetables, olive oil, butter, nuts, etc.

4. Eat only if you feel hungry

You must have read tip number 2 above. In the Ketogenic diet, eat when you are hungry. Do not eat when you are not feeling hungry. Let us elaborate why we are stressing this point again. Unnecessary snacking may become a mammoth issue in the Ketogenic diet. Some products are just so easily available and they are so tempting that you cannot resist them.

5. You can skip meals

Yes, you heard it right. You can even skip breakfast if you are not feeling hungry. This holds truth for any meal. When you are strictly following the Ketogenic diet, your hunger goes down significantly, especially if you have to lose a lot of weight. Your body is happily busy in burning excess fats and reduces your temptation to eat.

6. Wisely measure your development

Losing weight successfully might get trickier sometimes. If you focus on your weight all the time and step on the weighing scale all the time, you may get mislead. It de-motivates you and makes you anxious needlessly.

7. Be persistent

You would have all those chunks of fats around your waist and thighs in several years. So, how do you expect to lose all the extra fat in just a few weeks? If you want to shed that extra weight permanently, you have to make persistent efforts.

Keto Friendly Foods

Below are some examples of what food you should eat when you're on Ketogenic diet:

Fruits & Vegetables

- Asparagus
- Avocados
- Alfalfa sprouts
- Bell peppers
- Blueberries
- Blackberries
- Broccoli
- Coconut
- Carrot (In moderation)
- Cabbage
- Cranberries
- Cauliflower
- Celery
- Lemon
- Garlic (In moderation)
- Cucumbers

- Chicory
- Green beans
- Jicama
- Herbs
- Mushrooms
- Pumpkin
- Radishes
- Pickles
- Raspberries
- Salad greens
- Scallions
- Zucchini
- Tomatoes
- Strawberries
- Tomatoes
- Spaghetti squash (moderately)
- Okra
- Olives
- Limes
- Onions (In moderation)

Meats & Seafoods

*The Complete
Keto For Two Beginners Cookbook*

- Crab
- Beef
- Chicken
- Duck
- Goose
- Lamb
- Fish
- Octopus
- Mussels
- Lobsters
- Quail
- Sausage
- Pork
- Shrimp
- Scallops
- Venison
- Veal

Dairy

- Cottage cheese
- Burrito cheese

- Blue cheese dressing
- Cream cheese eggs
- Grilling cheese
- Greek yogurt (full-fat)
- Heavy whipping cream
- Halloumi cream
- Homemade whipped cream
- Mozzarella cheese
- Kefalotyri cheese
- Provolone cheese
- Queso blanco
- Ranch dressing
- Ricotta cheese
- Unsweetened almond milk
- Unsweetened coconut milk

Foods to Avoid On Keto Diet

Fruits & Vegetables

- Apricots
- Apples
- Bananas
- Artichokes
- Beans (all varieties)
- Boysenberries
- Butternut squash
- Burdock root
- Cantaloupe
- Cherries
- Chickpeas
- Corn
- Currants
- Edamame
- Egg plants
- Dates
- Elderberries
- Gooseberries

- Grapes
- Mangoes
- Leaks
- Huckleberries
- Honeydew melons
- Kiwifruit
- Parsnips
- Peaches
- Peas
- Potatoes
- Plums
- Pineapples
- Plantains
- Prune
- Raisins
- Taro
- Turnips
- Yams
- Winter squash
- Water chestnuts

Meat and Meats Alternative

- Sausage (with fillers)
- Hot dog (with fillers)
- Seitan
- Tofu
- Deli meat (Some not all)

Dairy

- Milk
- Almond milk (sweetened)
- Coconut milk (sweetened)
- Soy milk (regular)
- Yogurt (regular)

Nuts & Seeds

- Pistachios
- Cashew
- Chestnuts

Keto Pantry Essential

It is wise to have a well-stocked pantry when you are cooking keto meals. You do not need any exotic cooking ingredients; you just need to have the basics.

Keto Cooking Staples

1. Freshly ground black pepper

2. Ghee

3. Freshly ground pepper (clarified butter, without diary)

4. Olive oil

5. Grass-fed butter

In addition to this five staples, there are 10 perishable ingredients you will want to always have on hand; you just need to have the basics.

Keto Perishables

1. Avocados

2. Bacons (Uncured)

3. Eggs (pasture-raised, if you can)

4. Cream cheese (Full fat, or use a diary alternative)

5. Sour cream (Full fat, or use a diary alternative)

6. Cauliflower

7. Meat (Grass-fed, if you can)

8. Greens (Spinach, Kale or Arugula

9. Heavy whipping cream

10. Garlic (Fresh or pre-minced)

Keto Friendly Alternatives

You'd be surprised just how many carbs are in common everyday foods. Below is a chart of common foods and their keto-friendly alternatives that you can enjoy at any time.

The Complete
Keto For Two Beginners Cookbook

Note: Net carbs are the total carbs minus dietary fiber (soluble and insoluble) and sugar alcohols. Fiber and sugar alcohols are not counted toward net carbs because the human body cannot digest and break them down into glucose, so they do not spike blood sugar.

NOT SO FRIENDLY	NET CARBS	QUANTITY	KETO-FRIENDLY ALTERNATIVE	NET CARBS
Milk	13 grams	1 cup	Unsweetened almond milk	0 grams
Pasta	41 grams	1 cup	Zucchini noodles	3 grams
Wraps or tortillas	18 grams	1 medium	Low-carb tortillas	6 grams
Sugar	25 grams	2 tablespoons	Stevia or erythritol	0 grams
Rice	44 grams	1 cup	Shirataki rice	0 grams
Mashed potatoes	22 grams	½ cup	Mashed cauliflower	4 grams
Bread crumbs	36 grams	½ cup	Almond flour	6 grams
Soda	39 grams	12 ounces	Water, tea, or coffee	0 grams
French fries	44 grams	4 ounces	Zucchini fries	3 grams
Potato chips	46 grams	3½ ounces	Mixed nuts	14 grams

Testing for Ketosis

When you first start the keto diet, it's important to know if and when you're in ketosis when you first start eating low-carb. Not only is it a great confidence booster, but testing also lets you know that you're doing things right, or wrong, and whether you need to make any changes.

An easy test is to sniff for "keto-breath." After a few days, you might notice a taste that's somewhat fruity and a bit sour or even metallic. The reason for this? When your body is in ketosis, it creates the ketone bodies: acetone, acetoacetate, and beta-hydroxybutyrate. Acetone in particular is excreted through your urine and breath, which causes "keto-breath." This change in the smell of your breath and the taste in your mouth usually diminishes after a few weeks.

A more accurate way to tell is by using ketone urine test strips. They're fairly inexpensive and can instantly check the ketone levels in your urine. You can find them in packs of 100 for under $10 online or at most pharmacies. Try to take the test a few hours after you wake up in the morning, because being dehydrated after a night's sleep can cause a false positive.

The most accurate test involves a blood ketone meter. This type of test is a bit pricier at around $40 for the meter and up to $5 per test strip. The upside is it's much more accurate because it tests your blood directly. For nutritional ketosis, your reading should be between 0.5 and 5.0 millimeters. Long term, it's not necessary to continuously check on your ketone levels. Within a few weeks, you'll know if you're eating right, and it becomes very easy to stay in ketosis.

FAQS About Keto Diet

Here are some frequently asked questions about Keto diet.

Should I Count Net Carbs or Total carbs?

There's not a one-size-fits all approach, but what I typically recommend is counting net carbs for vegetables but total carbs for everything else. This recommendation is made because not all carbs are created equal, and some, like green vegetables should be include in your keto lifestyle. However, I don't encourage the consumption of other low-net-carbs processed foods like low-carb tortillas or Atkins bars.

What Should My Macronutrients be?

The macronutrient breakdown is typically 65 to 75 percent fat, 15 to 30 percent protein, and 5 to 10 percent carbohydrates. However, how this translates into grams of proteins carbohydrates and fats needs to be individualized for your body and your goals. I recommend counting macronutrients, especially in the beginning, to learn how best to formulate your diet. There are several online macro calculators that can be used at beginning.

Can I eat Too Much Fat?

Yes, you can definitely eat too much fat, and that is why it is important to follow an individualized macro breakdown. If your goal is fat loss, I recommend only eating fat until satiety. When following a keto lifestyle, your body's main fuel source will be fat, and this can come dietary fat or body fat. Your body will burn dietary fats first, because it is more readily available. If you are overeating dietary fat, you are giving your body no reason to burn body fat. Eating enough fat is good but overeating fat will not result in fat loss.

Do Calories Matter on a Keto Diet?

Yes, while there is more to fat loss and body recomposition than calories in versus calories out, calories do still matter. Eating too few or eating too many will prevent you from seeing results. Bothe the number of calories you eat and the types of foods that make up those calories will factor into you seeing results. Both the number of calories you eat and the types of foods that make up those calories will factor into you seeing results.

Can I substitute one cut of meat for Another-pork loin for Pork shoulder, for instance, or chicken breasts for chicken thighs?

Different meats have varying amount of connective tissue and fat, which means that they cook at different rates. Substituting one for another is usually possible. It just requires a shorter or longer cooking time.

Keto for Diabetics

If you have diabetes, a low-carb diet can still work for you. For type 2 diabetes, it can begin to reverse the condition; for type 1 diabetics, it can greatly improve blood sugar control. Always consult with your doctor before beginning a low-carb diet, especially with type 1 diabetes, because if you take medications, you may have to immediately decrease your doses. Your doctor may recommend doing a trial under their supervision so they can monitor your blood glucose levels and insulin doses. Additionally, for type 1 diabetes, you should eat over 50 grams of carbohydrates per day to prevent ketoacidosis.

Ketoacidosis is a toxic metabolic state that occurs when the body fails to regulate ketone production. The result is a severe accumulation of keto acids, which causes the pH of the blood to decrease substantially, making the blood more acidic. The most common causes for ketoacidosis are type 1 diabetes, prolonged alcoholism, and extreme starvation, which can result in diabetic ketoacidosis (DKA), alcoholic ketoacidosis, and starvation ketoacidosis, respectively. Ketoacidosis rarely occurs for reasons other than type 1 diabetics.

The chart below provides the carbohydrate contents of commonly eaten foods for reference (fats, fish, poultry, and meats don't contain carbs):

FOOD	SERVING SIZE	CARBS (GRAMS)	CALORIES
POTATO	1 large, baked, plain	56	283
RICE	1 cup, white or brown	50	223
OATMEAL	1 cup, dry	49	339
PINTO BEANS (COOKED)	1 cup	45	245
BAGEL	1 whole	44	245
YOGURT	1 cup, fruit-flavored, low-fat	42	225
CORN (COOKED)	1 cup	41	177
SPAGHETTI	1 cup	40	221
PIZZA	1 slice, cheese	39	290
APPLE JUICE	1 cup	28	113
SWEET POTATO	1 large	28	118
ORANGE JUICE	1 cup	26	112
ENGLISH MUFFIN	1 whole	25	130
WAFFLE	1 (7-inch diameter)	25	218
BANANA	1 medium	24	105

The Complete
Keto For Two Beginners Cookbook

FOOD	SERVING SIZE	CARBS (GRAMS)	CALORIES
APPLE	1 medium	21	81
CEREAL, READY TO EAT	1 cup	18	103
PANCAKE	1 (5-inch diameter)	15	90
MILK	1 cup	12	103
BREAD	1 slice, white	12	66
GREEN PEAS	½ cup	12	63
STRAWBERRIES	1 cup	11	45
CUCUMBER	1 (8-inch length)	9	47
YELLOW ONION	1 medium	8	44
BROCCOLI	1 stalk	6	51
ZUCCHINI	1 medium	4	33
CARROT	1 medium	4	25
TOMATO	1 medium	3	22
WHITE MUSHROOMS	1 cup	2	15
EGG	1 large	0.6	78
SPINACH	1 cup	0.4	7

Exercising in Keto

As you start your diet and the pounds fall off, think about how to lose more weight or get healthier to feel even better. This is a great time to become more active through exercise.

Increase the amount you exercise relative to what you do now. If you don't exercise at all, start taking short walks or slow jogs, or a combination of both, for 15 minutes every other day. If you already go to the gym or lift weights, add an extra exercise or start doing cardio. It doesn't matter what level you're at, try to do a little more than you're doing now. That's all it takes to become healthier. Exercise is incremental, and every increment is a boost to weight loss and feeling better.

If you have the time, try taking a class or doing an activity that involves moving, like a step class or dancing, or start playing a sport like basketball. It doesn't have to be competitive, nor do you need to be good or have any previous experience. Such activities are an easy way to get on your feet, and you can learn a new skill in the process.

Staying fit through regular physical activity has been proven to reduce blood pressure and cholesterol levels as well as reduce risk for various heart diseases and type 2 diabetes. In combination with the keto diet, your health will improve dramatically, and so will your energy levels. Any exercise, even if it's 15 minutes a week, is better than no exercise. Don't worry about how much you do in the beginning. Just start doing something and you'll build from there naturally.

Chapter Two: 21-Day Meal Plan

This is a sample menu for three weeks on a ketogenic diet plan.

Day 1

Breakfast – 1 hard-boiled egg; 1 slice of bacon; 1 shake with 1/2 cup of coconut milk and protein powder

Lunch – Breakfast Keto Muffins; 1 serving of cauliflower rice

Dinner – Skillet Shrimp and Sea Scallop with Scallions; 1 medium tomato

Dessert – Chocolate and Coconut Fudge Brownies

Day 2

Breakfast – Homemade Fluffy Tortillas with Cheese

Lunch – Saucy Cod with Mustard Greens Snack – Ranch Kale Chips

Dinner – Easy Spicy Meatballs; 1 keto dinner roll

DAY 3

Breakfast – Omelet with Vegetables and Mexican Cotija Cheese Snack – Caribbean-Style Chicken Wings

Lunch – Zucchini and Mushroom Lasagna; 1 handful of iceberg lettuce

Dinner – Asian-Style Fish Salad

Day 4

Breakfast – Classic Egg Salad Snack – Zucchini Parmesan Chips

Lunch – Rich Winter Beef Stew; 1 handful of mixed green salad with a few drizzles of a freshly squeezed lemon juice

Dinner – Easy Baked Halibut Steaks; 1 teaspoon of mustard

Day 5

Breakfast – Omelet with veggies; 1 slice of bacon

Lunch – Pork Cutlets with Spanish Onion; 1 serving of coleslaw

Dinner – Roasted Old Bay Prawns

Dessert – Classic Blueberry Cheesecake

Day 6

Breakfast – Scrambled eggs; 1 tomato; 1/2 cup of Greek-style yogurt

Lunch – Greek-Style Chicken Mélange; 1 serving of cauliflower rice

Dinner – Indian Cabbage Stir-Fry Dessert – Chocolate Chip Blondies

Day 7

Breakfast – Breakfast Keto Muffins; 1/2 cup of unsweetened almond milk

Lunch – Easiest Fish Jambalaya Ever; 1 serving of cabbage salad

Dinner – Spicy Glazed Eggplant; Pulled Pork with Mint and Cheese

Day 8

Breakfast – Frittata with Kale and Cheese

Lunch – Easy Creamy Broccoli Soup; 1 large tomato; 1 cup of fried mushrooms with 1 tablespoon of butter

Dinner – Cheesy Zucchini Fritters

Day 9

Breakfast – Bell Pepper Boats Snack – Greek-Style Pork Skewers with Sauce

Lunch – Authentic Thai Tom Kha Soup; 1/2 chicken breast; 1 scallion; 1/2 tomato

Dinner – Roasted Globe Artichokes with Cheese; a dollop of sour cream; 2 tablespoons tomato paste

Day 10

Breakfast – Breakfast Keto Muffins; 1/2 cup of unsweetened almond milk

Lunch – Easiest Fish Jambalaya Ever; 1 serving of cabbage salad

Dinner – Spicy Glazed Eggplant; Pulled Pork with Mint and Cheese

Day 11

Breakfast – 1 tablespoon of peanut butter; 1 slice of keto bread

Lunch – Cheese and Bacon Stuffed Chicken; 1 serving of cabbage salad

Dinner – Sea Bass with Vegetables and Dill Sauce

Day 12

Breakfast – Cauliflower Bites with Asiago Cheese

Lunch – Keto Tabbouleh Salad; Pork Loin Steaks in Creamy Pepper Sauce

Dinner – Favorite Chocolate Crepes

Day 13

Breakfast – Double Cheese Baked Stuffed Peppers

Lunch – Sunday Roast Beef with Herbs; 1 handful of baby spinach with 1 teaspoon of mustard and 1 teaspoon of olive oil

Dinner – Caprese Asparagus Salad

Dessert – Pecan Pie Chocolate Truffles

Day 14

Breakfast – Scrambled eggs; 1 tomato; 1/2 cup of Greek-style yogurt

Lunch – Warming Turkey and Leek Soup; 1 serving of roasted keto veggies

Dinner – Pulled Pork with Mint and Cheese; Spanish Ensalada de Pimientos Rojos

Day 15

Breakfast – Spicy Masala and Brown Mushroom Omelet

Snack – Tender Ribs with Hot Sauce

Lunch – Pork Medallions with Cabbage; 1 serving of low-carb grilled vegetables

Dinner – Beef Teriyaki Skillet; 1/2 cup of full-fat Greek yogurt

Day 16

Breakfast – 2 hard-boiled eggs; 2 slices of Cheddar cheese

Lunch – Swiss Cheese Soup; Grilled Turkey Drumsticks; 1 fresh bell pepper

Dinner – Mini Meatloaves with Spinach; 1 cucumber

Day 17

Breakfast – 2 hard-boiled eggs; 1/2 cup of Greek-style yogurt

Lunch – Mom's Festive Meatloaf

Dinner – Hungarian Fish Paprikash (Halászlé); Flourless Almond Butter Cookies

Dessert – Classic Chocolate Mousse

Day 18

Breakfast – Sunday Chicken Bake

Lunch – Rich and Easy Pork Ragout; 1 serving of steamed broccoli; 1 cucumber

Dinner – Sticky Barbecued Ribs; Broccoli Slaw with Tahini Dressing

Dessert – Chocolate and Coconut Fudge Brownies

Day 19

Breakfast – Nutty Cheesecakes Bowls

Lunch – Authentic Thai Tom Kha Soup; 1/2 grilled chicken breast

Dinner – Traditional Turkish Chicken Kebabs

Day 20

Breakfast – Sunday Chicken Bake

Lunch – Rich and Easy Pork Ragout; 1 serving of steamed broccoli; 1 cucumber

Dinner – Sticky Barbecued Ribs; Broccoli Slaw with Tahini Dressing

Dessert – Chocolate and Coconut Fudge Brownies

Day 21

Breakfast –1 hard-boiled egg; 1 slice of bacon; 1 serving of blue cheese

Lunch – Mexican-Style Beef Casserole; 1 serving of cabbage salad

The Complete
Keto For Two Beginners Cookbook

Snack – Skinny Cocktail Meatballs

Dinner – Chunky Pork Soup with Mustard Greens; Italian-Style Stuffed Peppers

Chapter Three: Snacks & Desserts

Zucchini Parmesan Chips

Preparation Time: 25 minutes

Serves: 2

Ingredients

- 1 tablespoon extra-virgin olive oil
- 1/4 teaspoon sea salt
- 1 teaspoon hot paprika
- 1/2-pound zucchini, sliced into rounds
- 2 tablespoons Parmesan cheese, grated

Directions

1. Gently toss the sliced zucchini with the olive oil, salt, and paprika. Place them on a tinfoil-lined baking sheet.

2. Sprinkle the Parmesan cheese evenly over each zucchini round. Bake in the preheated oven at 400 degrees F for 15 to 20 minutes or until your chips turns a golden-brown color.

Nutritional Information (per serving): Calories 52, Fat 4.6g, Carbs 1.4g, Protein 1.7g

Skinny Cocktail Meatballs

Preparation Time: 15 minutes

Serves: 2

Ingredients

- 1/4-pound ground turkey
- 1/4-pound ground pork
- 1-ounce bacon, chopped
- 1/4 cup flaxseed meal
- 1/2 teaspoon garlic, pressed
- 1 egg, beaten
- 1/2 cup cheddar cheese, shredded
- Sea salt, to season
- 1/4 teaspoon ground black pepper
- 1/4 teaspoon cayenne pepper
- 1/4 teaspoon marjoram

Directions

1. Start by preheating your oven to 395 degrees F.

2. Thoroughly combine all ingredients in a mixing bowl. Now, form the mixture into meatballs.

3. Place your meatballs in a parchment-lined baking sheet. Bake in the preheated oven for about 18 minutes, rotating the pan halfway through.

4. Serve with toothpicks and enjoy!

Nutritional Information: Calories 569, Fat 42.2g, Carbs 6.5g, Protein 40.1g

White Chocolate Butter Pecan Fat Bombs

Preparation time: 20 minutes

Makes: 4 bombs

Ingredients

- 1/4 tsp. vanilla extract
- 1 pinch Stevia
- 1 pinch salt
- 1/2 cup chopped pecans
- 2 tbsps. coconut oil
- 2 tbsps. butter
- 2 oz. cocoa butter
- 2 tbsps. powdered erythritol

Directions

1. In a small pan, melt coconut oil, cocoa butter and butter together until melted.

2. If you don't have powdered erythritol, you can easily make it. Stir in 2 tablespoons of powdered erythritol into the butter mixture until mixed.

3. Add a pinch of salt to bring out the sweetness.

4. Add in an optional pinch of Stevia to counteract the cooling effects of erythritol.

5. Add in vanilla extract.

6. Add a few chopped pecans in some silicon cupcake molds. I added about 3-4 pecans total to each mold, but this can be altered. If you don't have pecans, walnuts and hazelnuts work well with white chocolate too!

7. Pour your white chocolate mix evenly into the molds over the nuts and place in freezer immediately.

8. Freeze for about 30 minutes.

9. Serve!

Nutritional Information: Calories 287, Carbs 0.5g, Total Fat 30g, Protein 0.5g

Keto Lava Cake

Preparation time: 20 minutes

Serves: 1

Ingredients

- 1 tbsp. heavy cream
- 1/2 tsp vanilla extract
- 1/4 tsp. baking powder
- 1 pinch salt
- 2 tbsp. cocoa powder
- 1-2 tbsps. erythritol
- 1 medium egg

Directions

1. Preheat your oven to 350°F.

2. Combine your erythritol and cocoa powder and whisk to remove any clumps, in a bowl. Beat your egg until a little fluffy in another bowl.

3. Add your egg, heavy cream and vanilla extract to the erythritol and cocoa mixture, then add your salt and baking powder as well.

4. Spray a little cooking oil into the mug, pour your batter in and put it to bake for about 10-15 minutes at 350° F. The cake should not be overcooked to avoid having larva

5. Serve!

Nutritional Information: Calories 173, Carbs 4g, Total Fat 13g, Protein 8g

Low Carb Paleo Almond Flour Pie Crust

Preparation time: 15 minutes

Serves: 4 slices

Ingredients

- 1/4 cup Ghee (measured solid, then melted)
- 1 large Egg
- 1/2 tsp. Vanilla extract
- 2 1/2 cup Almond flour
- 1/3 cup Erythritol
- 1/4 tsp. Sea salt

Directions

1. Preheat the oven to 350 degrees F (177 degrees C).
2. Line the bottom of a 9 in (23 cm) round pie pan with parchment paper, or grease well.
3. Mix together the almond flour, erythritol, and sea salt in a large bowl.
4. Stir in the melted ghee and egg, until well mixed.
5. Stir vanilla into the melted ghee before adding to the dry ingredients.
6. Keep mixing, pressing and stirring, until the dough is uniform and there is no almond flour powder left. You can use a food processor to do this
7. Press the dough into the bottom of the prepared pan. Carefully poke holes in the surface using a fork to prevent bubbling.
8. Bake until lightly golden, about 12 minutes. (Add fillings after pre-baking)

The Complete
Keto For Two Beginners Cookbook

Nutritional Information: Calories 180, Carbs 5g, Total Fat 17g, Protein 6g

Keto Strawberry Mini Clafoutis

Preparation time: 30 minutes

Serves: 2

Ingredients

- ¼ (60 ml) cup unsweetened almond milk
- 1/2 tsp. sugar-free vanilla extract
- 2 (20 g/ 0.7 oz.) tbsps. powdered Erythritol or Swerve
- 1/2 cup + 2 tbsps. (62 g/ 2.2 oz.) almond flour
- 1/4 tsp. gluten-free baking powder
- 3-4 (70 g/ 2.5 oz.) sliced fresh strawberries
- 1 large egg
- 2 tbsps. (28 g/ 1 oz.) butter, ghee or virgin coconut oil, melted

Direction

1. In a medium bowl, place the egg, melted butter, almond milk and vanilla extract and beat until well mixed, then add the powdered Erythritol, almond flour and baking powder and beat again.

2. Divide the mixture between 2 ramekins (the ramekins I used are about 1 cup/ 240 ml each).

3. Top with sliced strawberries. Place in the oven and bake at 175 °C/ 350 °F for until set, about 25 minutes.

4. Remove from the oven and let it cool for a few minutes before serving.

5. Top with clotted cream, heavy whipping cream or coconut cream, to serve

Nutritional Information: Calories 347, Carbs 5.6g, Total Fat 30.6g, Protein 10.3g

Keto Chocolate Dairy Free Ice Cream

Preparation time: 10 minutes

Ingredients

- 1/3 cup Powdered erythritol
- 3 large egg yolks
- 1 teaspoon vanilla extract
- 1/3 cup LC Foods white sweetener - inulin
- 3 large egg yolks
- 1 teaspoon vanilla extract

Directions

1. Beat coconut cream, cocoa, and sweetener together in a medium saucepan.

2. Heat on medium heat until heated throughout.

3. Whisk yolks together in small bowl.

4. Slowly stream about 1/3-1/2 of the heated cocoa mixture into yolks while whisking in.

5. Return all the egg mixture to pot and continue heating on medium heat until thickened.

6. Stir in vanilla extract. Cool mixture in ice bath and process in ice cream machine once cooled.

Nutritional Information: Calories 186, Carbs 5g, Total Fat 17g, Protein 4g

No Bake Peanut Butter Protein Bars

Preparation time: 10 minutes

Serves: 2

Ingredients

- 1/2 cup powdered erythritol
- 2 cups chocolate chips of choice
- 1/2 cup coconut flour
- 2 scoops protein powder of choice
- 2 cups peanut butter

Directions

1. Line a deep pan with parchment paper and set aside. Use an 8 x 8-inch pan for thicker bars and any size bigger for thinner bars.

2. Add your dry ingredients and mix well in a large mixing bowl.

3. Melt your peanut butter with sticky sweetener in a small mixing bowl until combined. Add to dry ingredients and mix until fully combined.

4. Transfer peanut butter protein bar batter into the lined baking dish and press firmly in place. Refrigerate or freeze until firm. Cut into squares or bars once its firm and cover in optional chocolate and enjoy!

Nutritional Information: Calories 139, Carbs 6g, Total Fat 10g, Protein 8g

Keto Chocolate Dairy Free Ice Cream

Preparation time: 10 minutes

Serves: 2

Ingredients

- 1/3 cup Powdered erythritol
- 3 large egg yolks
- 1 teaspoon vanilla extract
- 1/3 cup LC Foods white sweetener - allulose
- 3 large egg yolks
- 1 teaspoon vanilla extract

Directions

7. Beat coconut cream, cocoa, and sweetener together in a medium saucepan.

8. Heat on medium heat until heated throughout.

9. Whisk yolks together in small bowl.

10. Slowly stream about 1/3-1/2 of the heated cocoa mixture into yolks while whisking in.

11. Return all the egg mixture to pot and continue heating on medium heat until thickened.

12. Stir in vanilla extract. Cool mixture in ice bath and process in ice cream machine once cooled.

Nutritional Information: Calories 186, Carbs 5g, Total Fat 17g, Protein 4g

Jalapeno Turkey Tomato Bites

Preparation time: 5 minutes

Serves: 2

Ingredients

- 2 tomatoes, sliced with a 3-inch thickness
- 1 cup turkey ham, chopped
- ¼ jalapeño pepper, seeded and minced
- 1/3 tbsp. Dijon mustard
- ¼ cup mayonnaise
- Salt and black pepper to taste
- 1 tbsp. parsley

Directions

1. Combine turkey ham, jalapeño pepper, mustard, mayonnaise, salt, and black pepper, in a bowl.

2. Arrange tomato slices in a single layer on a serving platter. Divide the turkey mixture between the tomato slices, garnish with parsley and serve.

Nutritional Information: Calories 245, Carbs 6.3g, Total Fat 15.3g, Protein 21g

Bell Pepper Boats

Preparation time: 15 minutes

Serves: 2

Ingredients

- 2 eggs
- 1/2 red onion, chopped
- 1/2 teaspoon garlic clove, minced
- 2 ounces canned boneless sardines, drained and chopped
- 1/4 freshly ground black pepper
- 1/2 cup tomatoes, chopped
- 1/4 cup mayonnaise
- 3 tablespoons Ricotta cheese
- 3 bell peppers, deveined and halved

Directions

1. Place the eggs and water in a saucepan; bring to a rapid boil; immediately remove from the heat. Allow it to sit, covered, for 10 minutes. Then, discard the shells, rinse the eggs under cold water, and chop them.

2. Thoroughly combine the onion, garlic, sardines, black pepper, tomatoes, mayonnaise, and cheese. Stuff the pepper halves and serve well chilled.

Nutritional Information: Calories 371, Carbs 6g, Total Fat 31.1g, Protein 16.2g

Party Spiced Cheese Chips

Preparation time: 18 minutes

Serves: 2

Ingredients

- 2 cups Monterrey Jack cheese, grated
- Salt to taste
- ½ tsp garlic powder
- ½ tsp cayenne pepper
- ½ tsp dried rosemary

Directions

1. Mix grated cheese with spices.
2. Create 2 tablespoons of cheese mixture into small mounds on a lined baking sheet.
3. Bake for about 15 minutes at 420 F; then allow to cool to harden the chips.

Nutritional Information: Calories 438, Carbs 1.8g, Total Fat 36.8g, Protein 27g

Hard-Boiled Eggs Stuffed with Ricotta Cheese

Preparation time: 30 minutes

Serves: 2

Ingredients

- 4 eggs
- 1 tbsp. green tabasco
- 2 tbsps. Greek yogurt
- 2 tbsps. ricotta cheese
- Salt to taste

Directions

1. Cover the eggs with salted water and bring to a boil over medium heat for 10 minutes.

2. Place the eggs in an ice bath and let cool for 10 minutes.

3. Peel and slice in half lengthwise. Scoop out the yolks to a bowl; mash with a fork. Whisk together the tabasco, Greek yogurt, ricotta cheese, mashed yolks, and salt, in a bowl.

4. Spoon this mixture into egg white. Arrange on a serving plate to serve.

Nutritional Information: Calories 173, Carbs 1.5g, Total Fat 312.5g, Protein 13.6g

Asparagus & Chorizo Traybake

Preparation time: 30 minutes

Serves: 2

Ingredients

- 2 tbsps. olive oil
- A bunch of asparagus, ends trimmed and chopped
- 4 oz. Spanish chorizo, sliced
- Salt and black pepper to taste
- ¼ cup chopped parsley

Directions

1. Preheat your oven to 325 F and grease a baking dish with olive oil.
2. Add in the asparagus and season with salt and black pepper.
3. Stir in the chorizo slices. Bake for 15 minutes until the chorizo is crispy.
4. Arrange on a serving platter and serve sprinkled with parsley.

Nutritional Information: Calories 411, Carbs 3.2g, Total Fat 36.5g, Protein 14.5g

Keto Pie Crust

Preparation time: 20 minutes

Serves: 2

Ingredients

- 100 g Butter (Cold)
- 1 Large Egg
- 2 tsps. White Vinegar
- 1 tbsp. Cream Cheese
- 3/4 Cup Almond Flour
- 1/3 Cup Coconut Flour
- 1/2 tsp. xanthan gum
- 1/4 tsp. Salt

Directions

1. Mix the almond flour, coconut flour, xanthan gum and salt together in a large glass bowl until each of the ingredients are indistinguishable.

2. Cut the cold butter up into small chunks, and add it to the dry ingredients (You should be very quick in doing this else it will not work).

3. Press the butter slowly into the dry ingredients by using two forks and do same too for the cream cheese.

4. Beat the egg in another bowl and pour it into the almond flour and butter mixture. Keep pressing this together with the forks, and add the vinegar to the mixture.

5. It will eventually resemble a slightly dry mixture. Grab it out of the bowl and slowly mix it together with your hands.

6. Wrap the mixture tightly in cling wrap and store in the fridge for at least 1 hour.

7. Roll the pie pastry between two pieces of baking paper when ready to bake. Place inside your pie pan, and blind bake with rice in the bottom for around 10-15 mins until the edges become brown.

8. Fill with any sort of filling (like my lemon curd) and let it set in the fridge.

Nutritional Information: Calories 135, Carbs 1.5g, Total Fat 12.5g, Protein 3g

Speedy Italian Appetizer Balls

Preparation time: 20 minutes

Serves: 2

Ingredients

- 2 oz. bresaola, chopped
- 2 oz. ricotta cheese, crumbled
- 2 tbsps. mayonnaise
- 6 green olives, pitted and chopped
- ½ tbsp. fresh basil, finely chopped

Directions

1. In a bowl, mix mayonnaise, bresaola and ricotta cheese.

2. Place in fresh basil and green olives. Form balls from the mixture and refrigerate. Serve chilled.

Nutritional Information: Calories 175, Carbs 1.1g, Total Fat 13.7g, Protein 11g

Quail Eggs & Prosciutto

Preparation time: 15 minutes

Serves: 2

Ingredients

- 3 thin prosciutto slices
- 9 basil leaves
- 9 quail eggs

Directions

1. Cover the quail eggs with salted water and bring to a boil over medium heat for 2-3 minutes.

2. Place the eggs in an ice bath and let cool for 10 minutes, then peel them.

3. Cut the prosciutto slices into three strips. Place basil leaves at the end of each strip.

4. Top with a quail egg. Wrap in prosciutto, secure with toothpicks and serve.

Nutritional Information: Calories 243, Carbs 0.5g, Total Fat 21g, Protein 12.5g

Tomato & Cheese in Lettuce Packets

Preparation time: 10 minutes

Serves: 2

Ingredients

- ¼ pound Gruyere cheese, grated
- ¼ pound feta cheese, crumbled
- ½ tsp oregano
- 1 tomato, chopped
- ½ cup buttermilk
- ½ head lettuce

Directions

1. In a bowl, mix feta and Gruyere cheese, oregano, tomato, and buttermilk.

2. Separate the lettuce leaves and put them on a serving platter.

3. Divide the mixture between them, roll up, folding in the ends to secure and serve.

Nutritional Information: Calories 433, Carbs 6.6g, Total Fat 32.5g, Protein 27.5g

Zucchini & Avocado Eggs with Pork Sausage

Preparation time: 20 minutes

Serves: 2

Ingredients

- ½ red onion, sliced
- 1 tsp canola oil
- 4 oz. pork sausage, sliced
- 1 cup zucchinis, chopped
- 1 avocado, pitted, peeled, chopped
- 3 eggs
- Salt and black pepper to season

Directions

1. Warm canola oil in a pan over medium heat and sauté the onion for 3 minutes.

2. Add the smoked sausage and cook for 3-4 minutes more, flipping once. Introduce the zucchinis, season lightly with salt, stir and cook for 5 minutes. Mix in the avocado and turn the heat off.

3. Create 3 holes in the mixture, crack the eggs into each hole, sprinkle with salt and black pepper, and slide the pan into the preheated oven and bake for 6 minutes until the egg whites are set or firm but with the yolks still runny.

Nutritional Information: Calories 402, Carbs 3.4g, Total Fat 31g, Protein 25g

Crab Salad Stuffed Avocado

Preparation time: 20 minutes

Serves: 2

Ingredients

- 1 avocado, peeled, halved lengthwise, and pitted
- ½ teaspoon freshly squeezed lemon juice
- 4½ ounces Dungeness crabmeat
- ½ cup cream cheese
- ¼ cup chopped red bell pepper
- ¼ cup chopped, peeled English cucumber
- ½ scallion, chopped
- 1 teaspoon chopped cilantro
- Pinch sea salt Freshly ground black pepper

Directions

1. Brush the cut edges of the avocado with the lemon juice and set the halves aside on a plate.

2. In a medium bowl, stir together the crabmeat, cream cheese, red pepper, cucumber, scallion, cilantro, salt, and pepper until well mixed.

3. Divide the crab mixture between the avocado halves and store them, covered with plastic wrap, in the refrigerator until you want to serve them, up to 2 days.

Nutritional Information: Calories 389, Carbs 10g, Total Fat 31g, Protein 19g

The Complete
Keto For Two Beginners Cookbook

Chapter Three: Breakfast & Smoothies Recipes

Scotch Eggs

Serves: 2

Preparation time: 30mins

Ingredients

- ½ c (50 g) breadcrumbs
- 2 tsp parsley
- Oil to fry in
- 9 eggs
- 9 oz. (400 g) sausage meat
- ½ c (50 g) breadcrumbs

Directions

1. Boil 8 eggs in hot water until hard.
2. Allow to cool and peel. Mix the sausage meat and the parsley.
3. Divide into eight portions and with your hand press flat on the counter.
4. For each serving, fully cover one egg with ground meat. Prepare two deep plates. Beat the remaining egg in one plate.
5. Add the breadcrumbs to the other plate. First coat the hardboiled eggs in egg, then the breadcrumbs.
6. Heat the oil in a pot or deep fryer and deep fry the Scotch Eggs for approx. 8 – 10 minutes.

7. Place on paper towel to remove grease and serve warm.

Nutritional Information: Calories 620, Fats 42g, Carbs 10.5g, Protein 23g

Rolled Smoked Salmon with Salmon & Cheese

Serves: 2

Preparation time: 10mins

Ingredients

- 2 tbsps. cream cheese, softened
- 1 lime, zested and juiced
- ½ avocado
- 1 tbsp. mint, chopped
- Salt to taste
- 2 slices smoked salmon

Directions

1. Mash the avocado with a fork in a bowl. Add in the cream cheese, lime juice, zest, mint, and salt and mix to combine.

2. Lay each salmon slice on a plastic wrap, spread with cream cheese mixture. Roll up the salmon and secure both ends by twisting.

3. Refrigerate for 2 hours, remove plastic, cut off both ends of each wrap, and cut wraps into half-inch wheels.

Nutritional Information: Calories 410, Fats 26g, Carbs 2.7g, Protein 38g

Breadless Breakfast Sandwich

Serves: 2

Preparation time: 10mins

Ingredients

- 2 eggs
- Salt and ground black pepper, to taste
- 2 tablespoons butter
- ¼ pound pork sausage, minced
- ¼ cup water
- 1 tablespoon guacamole

Directions

1. Mix minced sausage meat with some salt and pepper in a bowl, and stir well.

2. Shape a patty from this mixture and place it on a working surface.

3. Heat up a pan with 1 tablespoon butter over medium heat, add the sausage patty, fry for 3 minutes on each side, and transfer to a plate.

4. Crack an egg into 2 bowls and whisk them with some salt and pepper.

5. Heat up a pan with the rest of the butter over medium-high heat, place 2 biscuit cutters that you've greased with some butter in the pan and add an egg to each one.

6. Add the water to the pan, reduce heat, cover pan, and cook eggs for 3 minutes.

7. Transfer these egg "buns" to paper towels and drain the excess grease.

8. Place sausage patty on one egg "bun," spread guacamole over it, and top with the other egg "bun,"

Nutritional Information: Calories 200, Fats 9g, Carbs 5g, Protein 10g

Poultry Patties

Serves: 2

Preparation time: 20mins

Ingredients

- 1 lb. (500 g) mixed ground poultry
- 2 hard-boiled eggs
- 1 red onion
- 1 egg
- 3 Tbsp. (25 g) ground almonds
- Salt and pepper to taste

Directions

1. Peel the red onion and the two hard boiled eggs and chop finely.
2. Mix in the remaining ingredients and shape into small patties.
3. Sauté in a hot pan and enjoy warm or cold.

Nutritional Information: Calories 400, Fats 28.5g, Carbs 1.5g, Protein 31g

Broccoli, Egg & Pancetta Gratin

Serves: 2

Preparation time: 25 mins

Ingredients

- 1 head broccoli, cut into small florets
- 1 red bell pepper, seeded and chopped
- 4 slices pancetta, chopped
- 2 tsp olive oil
- 1 tsp dried oregano
- Salt and black pepper to taste
- 4 fresh eggs
- 4 tbsps. Parmesan cheese

Directions

1. Line a baking sheet with parchment paper and preheat the oven to 420 F.

2. Warm the olive oil in a frying pan over medium heat; cook the pancetta, stirring frequently, for about 3 minutes.

3. Arrange the broccoli, bell pepper, and pancetta on the baking sheet in a single layer, toss to combine; season with salt, oregano, and black pepper. Bake for 10 minutes until the vegetables have softened.

4. Remove, create four indentations with a spoon, and crack an egg into each one. Sprinkle with Parmesan cheese.

5. Return to the oven and bake for 5-7 minutes until the egg whites are firm and cheese melts.

Nutritional Information: Calories 464, Fats 38g, Carbs 4.2g, Protein 24g

Spinach Nests with Egg and Cheese

Serves: 2

Preparation time: 35 mins

Ingredients

- 1 tbsp. olive oil
- 1 tbsp. dried dill
- ½ lb. spinach, chopped
- 1 tbsp. pine nuts Salt and black pepper to taste
- ¼ cup feta cheese, crumbled
- 2 eggs

Directions

1. Sauté spinach in the olive oil over medium heat, to wilt for about 5 minutes, and season with salt and black pepper. Allow cooling.

2. Grease a baking sheet with cooking spray, mold 2 (firm and separate) spinach nests on the sheet, and crack an egg into each nest.

3. Top with feta cheese and scatter the dried dill over. Bake for 15 minutes at 350 F just until the egg whites have set and the yolks are still runny.

4. Plate the nests and serve right away sprinkled with pine nuts.

Nutritional Information: Calories 218, Fats 16.5g, Carbs 4.4g, Protein 12.3g

Avocado Shake

Serves: 2

Preparation time: 10mins

Ingredients

- 1 2/3 c (400 ml) milk
- 2/3 c (200 g) Greek yoghurt
- ½ lb. (200 g) avocado
- Salt and pepper to taste

Directions

1. Cut the avocado in half and scoop out the insides with a spoon.

2. Add all ingredients into a blender and blend at the highest setting for 3 minutes.

3. Season with salt and pepper to taste and divide into four portions.

Nutritional Information: Calories 215, Fats 15.7g, Carbs 10.5g, Protein 6.8g

Pesto Mug Sandwiches with Bacon & Ricotta

Serves: 2

Preparation time: 8 mins

Ingredients

- 2 eggs
- ¼ cup flax meal
- 2 tbsps. buttermilk
- 2 tbsps. pesto
- ¼ cup almond flour
- Salt and black pepper, to taste

Filling

- 2 tbsps. ricotta cheese
- 2 oz. bacon, sliced
- 1 avocado, sliced

Directions

1. Whisk eggs, buttermilk and pesto in a bowl. Season with salt and pepper.

2. Gently add in flax meal and almond flour and divide the mixture between two greased ramekins.

3. Place in the microwave and cook for 1-2 minutes. Leave to cool slightly before filling.

4. In a nonstick skillet over medium heat, cook the bacon until crispy, for about 5 minutes; set aside. Invert the cups onto a plate and cut in half, crosswise.

5. Assemble the sandwiches by spreading ricotta cheese and topping with bacon and avocado slices.

Nutritional Information: Calories 488, Fats 37g, Carbs 3.9g, Protein 17g

Quesadillas with Bacon & Mushrooms

Serves: 2

Preparation time: 30 mins

Ingredients

- 1 cup mushrooms, sliced
- 4 low carb tortilla shells
- 3 eggs, hard-boiled and chopped
- 2 tbsps. butter
- ½ cup cheddar cheese, grated
- 1 cup Swiss cheese, grated
- 3 oz. bacon
- 1 shallot, sliced

Directions

1. Fry the bacon in a skillet over medium heat for 4 minutes until the bacon is crispy.

2. Remove, chop and set aside. Sauté the shallot and mushrooms in the same grease for 5 minutes. Set aside. Melt 1 tablespoon of butter in a separate skillet over medium heat. Lay one tortilla in a skillet; sprinkle with some Swiss cheese.

3. Add some chopped eggs and bacon over the cheese, top with shallot, mushrooms, and sprinkle with cheddar cheese.

4. Cover with another tortilla shell.

5. Cook for 45 seconds, then carefully flip the quesadilla, and cook the other side too for 45 seconds.

6. Remove to a plate and repeat the cooking process using the remaining tortilla shells.

Nutritional Information: Calories 434, Fats 42.7g, Carbs 6.1g, Protein 27g

Ham & Cheese Keto Sandwiches

Serves: 2

Preparation time: 15 mins

Ingredients

- 4 eggs
- ½ tsp baking powder
- 5 tbsps. butter, at room temperature
- 4 tbsps. almond flour
- 2 tbsps. psyllium husk powder
- 2 slices mozzarella cheese
- 2 slices smoked ham

Directions

1. To make the buns, whisk together almond flour, baking powder, 4 tbsps. of butter, husk powder, and eggs in a bowl; mix until a dough forms.

2. Place the batter in two oven-proof mugs, and microwave for 2 minutes or until firm. Remove, flip the buns over and cut in half.

3. Place a slice of mozzarella cheese and a slice of ham on one bun half and top with the other. Warm the remaining butter in a skillet.

4. Add the sandwiches and grill until the cheese is melted and the buns are crispy.

Nutritional Information: Calories 516, Fats 145.2g, Carbs 2.3g, Protein 23.5g

Chili Avocado Boats

Serves: 2

Preparation time: 20 mins

Ingredients

- 1 tbsp. olive oil
- 2 avocados, halved and pitted, skin on
- ½ cup cheddar cheese, grated
- 2 eggs, beaten
- A pinch of chili powder
- Salt and black pepper, to taste
- 1 tbsp. fresh basil, chopped

Directions

1. In a mixing dish, mix cheese, chili powder, eggs, pepper, and salt.

2. Split the mixture equally into the avocado halves. Bake in the oven for 15 to 17 minutes at 360 F.

3. Decorate with basil before serving.

Nutritional Information: Calories 355, Fats 29g, Carbs 6.9g, Protein 12g

Breakfast Serrano Ham Frittata with Fresh Salad

Serves: 2

Preparation time: 22 mins

Ingredients

- 2 tbsps. extra virgin olive oil
- 3 slices serrano ham, chopped
- 1 tomato, cut into 1-inch chunks
- 1 cucumber, sliced
- 1 small red onion, sliced
- 1 tbsp. balsamic vinegar
- 4 eggs
- 1 cup Swiss chard, chopped
- Salt and black pepper to taste
- 1 green onion, sliced

Directions

1. Whisk the vinegar, 1 tbsp. of olive oil, salt, and pepper to make the dressing; set aside.

2. Combine the tomato, red onion, and cucumber in a salad bowl, drizzle with the dressing and toss the veggies.

3. Sprinkle with the serrano ham and set aside.

4. Crack the eggs into a bowl and whisk together with salt and pepper; set aside.

5. Heat the remaining olive oil in the cast iron pan over medium heat.

6. Sauté the onion for 3 minutes.

7. Add the Swiss chard to the skillet, season with salt and pepper, and cook for 2 minutes. Pour the egg mixture all over the Swiss chard, reduce the heat to medium-low, cover, and cook for 4 minutes.

8. Transfer the pan to the oven. Bake to brown on top for 5 minutes at 390 F. Cut the frittata into wedges and serve with the prepared salad.

Nutritional Information: Calories 364, Fats 26.3g, Carbs 4.7g, Protein 20.2g

Microwave Bacon Mug Eggs

Serves: 2

Preparation time: 5 mins

Ingredients

- 4 eggs
- 4 tbsps. coconut milk
- ½ cup bacon, cubed
- ½ tsp oregano
- Salt and black pepper, to taste
- 1 spring onion, sliced

Directions

1. In a bowl, crack the eggs and beat until combined; season with salt and black pepper.

2. Add coconut milk, bacon, spring onion, and oregano. Pour the mixture into two microwave-safe cups.

3. Transfer to the microwave and cook for 1 minute. Serve warm.

Nutritional Information: Calories 370, Fats 17.5g, Carbs 1.9g, Protein 23.7g

Peanut Butter & Pastrami Gofres

Serves: 2

Preparation time: 20 mins

Ingredients

- 4 eggs
- ½ tsp baking soda
- 2 tbsps. peanut butter, melted
- 4 tbsps. coconut flour
- ¼ tsp salt
- ½ tsp dried rosemary
- 3 tbsps. tomato puree
- 4 ounces pastrami, chopped

Directions

1. Preheat closed waffle iron to high.

2. In a mixing bowl, whisk eggs with rosemary and salt. Stir in coconut flour, baking soda, and peanut butter.

3. To the waffle iron, add in a third of the batter and cook for 3 minutes until golden.

4. Repeat with the remaining batter.

5. To serve, spread the tomato puree over each gofre and top with chopped pastrami.

Nutritional Information: Calories 411, Fats 27g, Carbs 4.2g, Protein 25.6g

Lettuce Wraps

Serves: 2

Preparation time: 10mins

Ingredients

- 8 leaves of lettuce
- 7 Tbsp. (100 g) chive & onion cream cheese
- 4 radishes

Directions

1. Wash the radishes and dice fine. Then mix in with the chive & onion cream cheese.

2. Spread the filling evenly on the lettuce. Roll up the leaves of lettuce and serve two per person.

Nutritional Information: Calories 84, Fats 6.1g, Carbs 1.2g, Protein 5.7g

Breakfast Blueberry Coconut Smoothie

Serves: 2

Preparation time: 5 mins

Ingredients

- 1 avocado, pitted and sliced
- 2 cups blueberries
- 1 cup coconut milk
- 6 tbsps. coconut cream
- 2 tsp erythritol
- 2 tbsps. coconut flakes

Directions

1. Combine the avocado slices, blueberries, coconut milk, coconut cream, erythritol, and ice cubes in a smoothie maker and blend until smooth.

2. Pour the smoothie into drinking glasses, and serve sprinkled with coconut flakes.

Nutritional Information: Calories 492, Fats 36.3g, Carbs 8.6g, Protein 9.6g

Chorizo Sausage Egg Cakes

Serves: 2

Preparation time: 15 mins

Ingredients

- 1 tsp butter, melted
- 4 eggs, beaten
- Salt and black pepper, to taste
- 1 cup mozzarella cheese, grated
- 2 chorizo sausages, cooked and chopped
- 1 tbsp. parsley, chopped

Directions

1. In a bowl, stir the eggs, sausages and cheese; season with salt and pepper.

2. Add into greased with butter muffin cups, and bake in the oven for 8-10 minutes at 400 F. Sprinkle with parsley to serve.

Nutritional Information: Calories 512, Fats 35.5g, Carbs 5.4g, Protein 41g

Morning Herbed Eggs

Serves: 2

Preparation time: 15 mins

Ingredients

- 1 spring onion, finely chopped
- 2 tbsps. butter
- 1 tsp fresh thyme
- 4 eggs
- ½ tsp sesame seeds
- 2 garlic cloves, minced
- ½ cup parsley, chopped
- ½ cup sage, chopped
- ¼ tsp cayenne pepper
- Salt and black pepper, to taste

Directions

1. Melt butter in a non-stick skillet over medium heat.

2. Add garlic, parsley, sage and thyme and cook for 30 seconds.

3. Carefully crack the eggs into the skillet. Lower the heat and cook for 4-6 minutes.

4. Adjust the seasoning. When the eggs are just set, turn the heat off and transfer to a serving plate.

5. Drizzle the cayenne pepper and sesame seeds on top of the egg.

6. Top with spring onions and serve.

Nutritional Information: Calories 283, Fats 22.3g, Carbs 5.3g, Protein 13.3g

Power Green Smoothie

Serves: 2

Preparation time: 5 mins

Ingredients

- 1 cup collard greens, chopped
- 3 stalks celery, chopped
- 1 ripe avocado, skinned, pitted, sliced
- 1 cup ice cubes
- 2 cups spinach, chopped
- 1 large cucumber, peeled and chopped
- Chia seeds to garnish

Directions

1. Add the collard greens, celery, avocado, and ice cubes in a blender, and blend for 50 seconds.

2. Add the spinach and cucumber, and process for another 40 seconds until smooth. Transfer the smoothie into glasses, garnish with chia seeds and serve right away.

Nutritional Information: Calories 187, Fats 12g, Carbs 7.6g, Protein 3.2g

Spinach Blueberry Smoothie

Serves: 2

Preparation time: 5 mins

Ingredients

- 1 cup coconut milk
- 1 cup spinach
- ½ English cucumber, chopped
- ½ cup blueberries
- 1 scoop plain protein powder
- 2 tablespoons coconut oil
- 4 ice cubes Mint sprigs, for garnish

Directions

1. Put the coconut milk, spinach, cucumber, blueberries, protein powder, coconut oil, and ice in a blender and blend until smooth.

2. Pour into 2 glasses, garnish each with the mint, and serve immediately.

Nutritional Information: Calories 353, Fats 32g, Carbs 9g, Protein 15g

Peanut Butter Cup Smoothie

Serves: 2

Preparation time: 5 mins

Ingredients

- 1 cup water
- ¾ cup coconut cream
- 1 scoop chocolate protein powder
- 2 tablespoons natural peanut butter
- 3 ice cubes

Directions

1. Put the water, coconut cream, protein powder, peanut butter, and ice in a blender and blend until smooth.

2. Pour into 2 glasses and serve immediately.

Nutritional Information: Calories 486, Fats 40g, Carbs 11g, Protein 30g

Lemon Cashew Smoothie

Serves: 1

Preparation time: 5 mins

Ingredients

- 1 cup unsweetened cashew milk
- ¼ cup heavy (whipping) cream
- ¼ cup freshly squeezed lemon juice
- 1 scoop plain protein powder
- 1 tablespoon coconut oil
- 1 teaspoon sweetener

Directions

1. Put the cashew milk, heavy cream, lemon juice, protein powder, coconut oil, and sweetener in a blender and blend until smooth.

2. Pour into a glass and serve immediately.

Nutritional Information: Calories 503, Fats 45g, Carbs 15g, Protein 29g

The Complete
Keto For Two Beginners Cookbook

Yummy Blue Cheese & Mushroom Omelet

Serves: 2

Preparation time: 15 mins

Ingredients

- 4 eggs, beaten
- 4 button mushrooms, sliced
- Salt, to taste
- 1 tbsp. olive oil
- ½ cup blue cheese, crumbled
- 1 tomato, thinly sliced
- 1 tbsp. parsley, chopped

Directions

1. Set a pan over medium heat and warm the oil.
2. Sauté the mushrooms for 5 minutes until tender; season with salt.
3. Add in the eggs and cook as you swirl them around the pan using a spatula.
4. Cook eggs until partially set.
5. Top with cheese; fold the omelet in half to enclose filling.
6. Decorate with tomato and parsley and serve warm.

Nutritional Information: Calories 310, Fats 25g, Carbs 1.5g, Protein 18.5g

Roasted Stuffed Avocados

Serves: 2

Preparation time: 13 mins

Ingredients

- 2 large avocados, halved and pitted
- 4 eggs
- 1 tbsp. Parmesan cheese, grated
- Salt and black pepper to season
- 1 tbsp. parsley, chopped to garnish

Directions

1. Grease a baking dish with cooking spray.

2. Crack each egg into each avocado half, season with salt and black pepper, and place them on the baking sheet.

3. Top with Parmesan cheese.

4. Bake the filled avocados in the oven for 8 or 10 minutes at 380 F or until eggs are cooked and cheese is melted.

5. Garnish with parsley.

Nutritional Information: Calories 468, Fats 39.1g, Carbs 6.2g, Protein 17.2g

Asparagus & Goat Cheese Frittata

Serves: 2

Preparation time: 20 mins

Ingredients

- 1 tbsp. olive oil
- ½ onion, chopped
- 1 cup asparagus, chopped
- 4 eggs, beaten
- ½ tsp habanero pepper, minced
- Salt and red pepper, to taste
- ¾ cup goat cheese, cut into chunks
- ½ tbsp. basil pesto
- 1 tbsp. parsley, to serve

Directions

1. Preheat oven to 370 F. Sauté onion in warm olive oil over medium heat until caramelized.

2. Place in the asparagus and cook until tender, about 5 minutes.

3. Add in habanero pepper and eggs; season with red pepper and salt.

4. Cook until the eggs are set. Scatter goat cheese over the frittata.

5. Transfer to the oven and cook for approximately 12 minutes, until the frittata is set in the middle.

6. Slice into wedges and decorate with parsley before serving.

Nutritional Information: Calories 345, Fats 27g, Carbs 5.2g, Protein 21.6g

Golden Turmeric Latte with Nutmeg

Serves: 2

Preparation time: 7 mins

Ingredients

- 2 cups almond milk
- 1/3 tsp cinnamon powder
- ½ cup brewed coffee
- ¼ tsp turmeric powder
- 1 tsp xylitol
- Nutmeg powder to garnish

Directions

1. Add the almond milk, cinnamon powder, coffee, turmeric, and xylitol in the blender.

2. Blend the ingredients at medium speed for 50 seconds and pour the mixture into a saucepan.

3. Over low heat, set the pan and heat through for 6 minutes, without boiling. Keep swirling the pan to prevent from boiling.

4. Turn the heat off, and serve in latte cups, topped with nutmeg powder.

Nutritional Information: Calories 153, Fats 13.2g, Carbs 0.9g, Protein 3.9g

Strawberry Chia Seed Pudding in Glass Jars

Serves: 2

Preparation time: 10 mins + chilling time

Ingredients

- 1 tsp vanilla extract
- 1 cup water
- 2 tbsps. chia seeds
- 2 tbsps. flax seed meal
- 4 tbsps. almond meal
- ½ tsp granulated stevia
- 2 tbsps. walnuts, chopped
- 4 mint leaves, chopped
- ½ cup strawberries, mashed

Directions

1. Place chia seeds, flaxseed meal, almond meal, strawberries, and granulated stevia in a bowl and pour over the water. Stir in vanilla.

2. Refrigerate for at least 2 hours or overnight.

3. When the pudding is ready, spoon into glass jars, sprinkle with walnuts and mint serve warm.

Nutritional Information: Calories 275, Fats 19g, Carbs 4.5g, Protein 14g

Sausage Cakes with Poached Eggs

Serves: 2

Preparation time: 20 mins

Ingredients

- ½ pound sausage patties
- 1 tbsp. olive oil
- 2 tbsps. guacamole
- ½ tsp vinegar
- Salt and black pepper to taste
- 2 eggs
- 1 tbsp. cilantro, chopped

Directions

1. Fry the sausage patties in warm oil over medium heat until lightly browned, about 6-8 minutes. Remove the patties to a plate.

2. Spread the guacamole on the sausages. Boil the vinegar with 2 cups of water in a pot over high heat, and reduce to simmer, without boiling.

3. Crack each egg into a small bowl and gently put the egg into the simmering water; poach for 2 to 3 minutes.

4. Use a perforated spoon to remove from the water on a paper towel to dry.

5. Repeat with the other egg. Top each stack with a poached egg, sprinkle with cilantro, salt, and black pepper to serve.

Nutritional Information: Calories 523, Fats 43g, Carbs 2.5g, Protein 28g

Lettuce Cups Filled Mushrooms & Cheese

Serves: 2

Preparation time: 20 mins

Ingredients

- 1 tbsp. olive oil
- ½ onion, chopped
- Salt and black pepper, to taste
- ½ cup mushrooms, chopped
- ¼ tsp cayenne pepper
- 2 fresh lettuce leaves
- 2 slices gruyere cheese
- 1 tomato, sliced

Directions

1. Warm the olive oil in a pan over medium-high heat.
2. Sauté the onion for 3 minutes, until soft.
3. Stir in the mushrooms and cayenne and cook for 4-5 minutes until tender.
4. Season with salt and pepper. Spoon the mushroom mixture into the lettuce leaves, top with tomato and cheese slices to serve.

Nutritional Information: Calories 481, Fats 42g, Carbs 5.7g, Protein 20g

Chapter Five: Poultry Recipes

Keto Chicken Tenders

Preparation time: 30 minutes

Serves: 2

Ingredients

- 2 eggs beaten
- 1 lb. chicken tenderloin about 8
- low carb ketchup
- ½ cup almond flour
- ¼ cup flaxseed meal
- ¼ tsp paprika
- salt and pepper

Directions

1. Preheat the oven to 375F.
2. Combine almond flour, flaxseed meal, paprika, salt and pepper in a bowl.
3. In a separate bowl, add the beaten eggs.
4. Dip a chicken tenderloin into the egg, turn to coat and drop it into the dry mixture.
5. Coat thoroughly then place it on a baking sheet lined with a silicone mat. Continue with the rest of the tenderloins.

6. Bake until the chicken is cooked through, about 25 minutes.

7. Serve with low carb ketchup.

Nutritional Information: Calories 587, Carbs 12g, Total Fat 32g, Protein 63g

Paleo garlic chicken nuggets recipe

Preparation time: 15 minutes

Serves: 2

Ingredients

- 2 Tablespoons garlic powder
- 1/4-1/2 cup ghee
- 2 chicken breasts, cut into cubes
- 1/2 cup coconut flour
- 1 egg
- Salt to taste

Directions

1. Mix the coconut flour, garlic powder, and salt together in a bowl. In a separate bowl, whisk 1 egg to make the egg wash.

2. In a saucepan on medium heat, place the ghee. Dip the cubed chicken in the egg wash and then drop into the coconut flour mixture to coat it with the "breading."

3. Place some of the "breaded" chicken cubes carefully into the ghee and fry until golden, about 10 minutes. Ensure there's only a single layer of chicken in the pan so that they can all cook in the oil.

4. Turn the chicken pieces to make ensure they get cooked uniformly. This can be done in batches depending on the size of the pan

5. Place the cooked chicken pieces onto paper towels to soak up any excess oil.

6. Serve with some Paleo ketchup.

Clarion Ulreich

Nutritional Information: Calories 665, Carbs 17g, Total Fat 38g, Protein 55g

Asian chicken wraps with tahini tamari sauce

Preparation time: 10 minutes

Serves: 2

Ingredients

- 1/2 zucchini, shredded
- 2 Tablespoons cilantro leaves
- Coconut oil or olive oil or avocado oil to coconut the chicken in
- 1 Tablespoon tahini paste
- 1/2 Tablespoon tamari sauce
- Romaine lettuce leaves
- 1 chicken breast, cut into long strips
- 1/2 bell pepper, cut into long strips
- 1/2 cucumber, peeled and cut into long strips

Directions

1. Put oil in a fry pan and fry the chicken breast strips until they're cooked.

2. Cut the vegetables into long strips as well.

3. Make the sauce by Mix the tahini paste and the tamari sauce together in a small bowl or cup, to make sauce.

4. Place everything on a large plate and serve with lettuce leaves as wraps

Nutritional Information: Calories 250, Carbs 12g, Total Fat 20g, Protein 23g

Chicken Thighs with Pan Gravy

Preparation time: 30 minutes

Serves: 2

Ingredients

- 3 medium Chicken Thighs (~15 oz.)
- 1 tbsp. Olive Oil
- 1 tbsp. Wayward Gourmet Nobody Calls Me Chicken
- Salt and Pepper to Taste
- 1/3 cup Heavy Cream
- 1/4 tsp. Xanthan Gum

Directions

1. Season each chicken thigh with salt, pepper, and 1 tsp. Wayward Gourmet seasoning per thigh.

2. Heat 1 tbsp. Olive Oil into a pan over medium-high heat. Place chicken thighs in the pan, skin side down and cook for about 7-8 minutes.

3. Flip chicken thighs and cook for about 8-10 minutes on medium-low heat or until chicken is cooked. Remove chicken from pan.

4. Turn heat back up to medium and add heavy cream to the pan. Stir cream vigorously as it starts to thicken. Once it thickens some, add xanthan gum to the pan and mix it in well. Once your gravy thickens completely, spoon over chicken thighs and serve.

Nutritional information: Calories 364, Carbs 0.7 g, Total Fat 31.7g, Protein 19.7g

The Complete
Keto For Two Beginners Cookbook

Protein Pancakes

Preparation time: 5 minutes

Serves: 2

Ingredients

- 2 Large Eggs
- 2 ounces of Cream Cheese
- 20 Drops of Stevia

Directions

1. Add butter to a pan at medium heat. In a medium bowl, combine all of the ingredients.

2. Mix well with a fork until the ingredients are well combined should resemble batter. Let batter sit for 1-2 minutes.

3. Pour batter into pan and flip twice cooking both sides equally.

Nutritional Information: Calories 97, Total Fat 8.3g, Carbs 1.1g, Protein 5g

Jalapeno Popper Scrambled Eggs

Preparation time: 10 minutes

Serves: 1

Ingredients

- 1 oz. Cream Cheese
- 1/4 tsp. Garlic Powder
- 1/4 tsp. Onion Powder
- 2 large Eggs
- 1 slice Bacon, chopped
- 1 medium Jalapeno Pepper
- Salt and Pepper to Taste

Directions

1. Fry bacon over medium heat until crisp. De-seed and chop jalapeno pepper.

2. Add to pan to cook until soft. Crack eggs into the pan and lightly scramble. Turn off stove's heat.

3. Add spices and cream cheese. Stir together.

Nutritional Information: Calories 97, Total Fat 8.3g, Carbs 1.1g, Protein 5g

Teriyaki Turkey Bowls

Preparation time: 15 minutes

Serves: 2

Ingredients

- 3/4-pound lean ground turkey
- 1 brown onion, chopped
- 1 red bell pepper, deveined and chopped
- 1 serrano pepper, deveined and chopped
- 1 tablespoon rice vinegar
- 1 garlic clove, pressed
- 1 tablespoon sesame oil
- 1/2 teaspoon ground cumin
- 1/2 teaspoon hot sauce
- 2 tablespoons peanut butter
- Sea salt and cayenne pepper, to season
- 1/2 teaspoon celery seeds
- 1/2 teaspoon mustard seeds
- 1 rosemary sprig, leaves chopped
- 2 tablespoons fresh Thai basil, snipped

Directions

1. Heat a medium-sized pan over medium-high heat; once hot, brown the ground turkey for 4 to 6 minutes; reserve.

2. Then cook the onion and peppers in the pan drippings for a further 2 to 3 minutes.

3. Add 1/4 cup of cold water to another saucepan and heat over medium heat. Now, stir in vinegar, garlic, sesame oil, cumin, hot sauce, peanut butter, salt, cayenne pepper, celery seeds, and mustard seeds. Let it simmer, stirring occasionally, until the mixture begins to bubble slightly.

4. Bring the mixture to a boil; then, immediately remove from the heat and add the cooked ground turkey and sautéed onion/pepper mixture.

5. Ladle into serving bowls and garnish with the rosemary and Thai basil. Enjoy!

Nutritional Information: Calories 410, Total Fat 27.1g, Carbs 27.1g, Protein 36.5g

Breakfast Pizza

Preparation time: 16 minutes

Serves: 2

Ingredients

- 10 Slices Pepperoni
- Salt, Pepper, Garlic Powder and Onion Powder to taste
- 4 Eggs
- 4 Slices Bacon
- 2 Oz. Cheddar Cheese

Directions

1. Cook the bacon and reserve the bacon grease in the skillet
2. Let the pan cool slightly, then crack four eggs into the pan, try to put them close together
3. Apply seasoning and cook in the oven at 450 for 6 minutes
4. Add the cheddar and toppings and cook for another 4 minutes
5. Put bacon on top and serve

Nutritional Information: Calories 207, Total Fat 24g, Carbs 1g, Protein 22g

Chicken Nuggets

Preparation time: 20 minutes

Serves: 2

Ingredients

- ½ tsp Baking Powder
- 1 egg
- 1 Tbsp. Water
- 1 Chicken Breast
- ½ Oz. Grated Parmesan
- 2 Tbsp. Almond Flour

Directions

1. Start by heating your deep fryer to 375 degrees
2. Cook a chicken breast and cut into cubes
3. Mix the grated parmesan, almond flour, and baking powder
4. Add the egg and whisk
5. Add the water and whisk
6. Roll the chicken breasts in the batter until they are fully coated, then use a fork to drop them into the frying oil
7. Cook until the batter turns golden brown, approximately 5 minutes

Nutritional Information: Calories 166, Total Fat 8g, Carbs 1g, Protein 23g

Mighty Meaty Pizza

Preparation time: 30 minutes

Serves: 2

Ingredients

- 20 oz. Ground Beef
- 2 Large Eggs
- ½ cup Cheddar Cheese, shredded
- 28 Pepperoni Slices
- ½ cup pizza sauce
- 4 oz. Mozzarella Cheese

Directions

1. Take ground beef and add eggs and seasoning, mix it together
2. Place ground beef into cast iron skillet, form into pizza crust
3. Cook for 15 minutes, or until meat is done
4. Take out the crust and add sauce, cheese and toppings
5. Cook for additional time until the cheese is fully melted

Nutritional Information: Calories 610, Total Fat 45g, Carbs 2g, Protein 44g

Bacon Cheddar Omelette

Preparation time: 10 minutes

Serves: 2

Ingredients

- 2 large Eggs
- 1 oz. Cheddar Cheese
- 2 stalks Chives
- Salt and Pepper to Taste
- 2 slices Bacon, already cooked
- 1 tsp. Bacon Fat

Directions

1. Make sure all ingredients are prepped. Heat a pan on medium-low with bacon fat in.

2. Add the eggs, and season with chives, salt, and pepper. Once the edges are starting to set, add your bacon to the center and let cook for 20-30 seconds. Turn off the stove.

3. Add the cheese on top of the bacon, and fold edges on top of the cheese like a burrito. Flip over and warm through on the other side.

Nutritional Information: Calories 610, Total Fat 39g, Carbs 1g, Protein 24g

Spinach Onion Goat Cheese Omelette

Preparation time: 10 minutes

Serves: 2

Ingredients

- 3 large Eggs
- 2 tbsp. Heavy Cream
- 1 oz. Goat Cheese
- Salt and pepper to Taste
- 1/4 medium Onion
- 2 tbsp. Butter
- 1 large Handful of Spinach

Directions

1. Slice onion into long strips. Sauté in butter until caramelized.

2. Add spinach to pan and allow to wilt. Remove vegetables from the pan.

3. Mix 3 large eggs, cream, and salt and pepper together in a container.

4. Pour egg mixture into the pan and allow to cook over medium-low heat. Once edges of omelette begin to set, spoon spinach and onions over 1/2 of the omelette.

5. Crumble goat cheese over the spinach. As the top of the omelette begins to set, fold over the omelette.

Nutritional Information: Calories 620, Total Fat 56g, Carbs 5.5g, Protein 25g

Low Carb Buffalo Chicken Meatballs

Preparation time: 20 minutes

Serves: 2

Ingredients

- 2 tablespoons prepared ranch dressing plus more for serving
- 1 tablespoon dry ranch seasoning
- 1/4 cup hot sauce plus more for serving
- 1 egg
- 1-pound ground chicken or turkey
- 1/2 cup almond flour
- 1/4 cup grated cheddar cheese

Directions

1. Preheat oven to 500 degrees and line baking sheet with parchment paper.
2. In a medium bowl, place all of the ingredients mix well with your hands.
3. Form mixture into 9 evenly sized meatballs and place on the prepared baking sheet.
4. Bake for 15 minutes or until cooked through.
5. Serve with extra hot sauce and ranch dressing, as desired

Nutritional Information: Calories 156, Total Fat 11g, Carbs 2g, Protein 12g

Chicken Wings with Lemons & Capers

Preparation time: 30 minutes

Serves: 2

Ingredients

- 2 tbsps. butter
- 1 cup chicken broth
- 1 tsp garlic powder
- 1 tsp lemon zest
- 3 tbsps. lemon juice
- ½ tsp cilantro, chopped
- 1 tbsp. soy sauce
- ¼ tsp xanthan gum
- 3 tbsps. xylitol
- 1-pound chicken wings
- Salt and black pepper, to taste
- ¼ cup capers

Directions

1. Heat a saucepan over medium heat and add lemon juice and zest, soy sauce, cilantro, chicken broth, xylitol, and garlic powder.

2. Bring to a boil, cover, lower the heat, and let simmer for 10 minutes. Stir in the butter, capers, and xanthan gum.

3. Set aside. Season the wings with salt and black pepper. Preheat grill to high heat and cook the chicken wings for 5 minutes per side. Serve topped with the sauce.

Nutritional Information: Calories 343, Total Fat 24.6g, Carbs 3.6g, Protein 19.5g

Creamy Chicken with Pancetta, Mushrooms & Spinach

Preparation time: 50 minutes

Serves: 2

Ingredients

- 1-pound chicken thighs
- Salt and black pepper, to taste
- 1 onion, chopped
- 1 tbsp. coconut oil
- 4 pancetta strips, chopped
- 2 garlic cloves, minced
- 1 cup white mushrooms, halved
- 1 cup spinach
- 2 cups white wine
- 1 cup whipping cream
- 2 tbsps. parsley, chopped

Directions

1. Cook the pancetta in a pan over medium heat until crispy, for about 4-5 minutes; remove to paper towels.

2. To the pancetta fat, add the coconut oil and chicken, sprinkle with black pepper and salt and cook until brown.

3. Remove to paper towels too. In the same pan, sauté the onion and garlic for 4 minutes. Then, mix in the mushrooms and cook for another 5 minutes. Return the pancetta and browned chicken to the pan.

4. Stir in the wine and bring to a boil, reduce the heat, and simmer for 20 minutes.

5. Pour in the whipping cream and spinach and warm without boiling.

6. Scatter over the parsley and serve.

Nutritional Information: Calories 353, Total Fat 17.5g, Carbs 5.2g, Protein 22.3g

Creamy Mushroom & White Wine Chicken

Preparation time: 36 minutes

Serves: 2

Ingredients

- 1 tbsp. butter
- 1 tbsp. olive oil
- 1-pound chicken breasts, cut into chunks
- Salt and black pepper to taste
- 1 packet white onion soup mix
- 2 cups chicken broth
- ¼ cup white wine
- 15 baby bella mushrooms, sliced
- 1 cup heavy cream
- 2 tbsps. parsley, chopped

Directions

1. Add butter and olive oil in a saucepan and heat over medium heat.

2. Season the chicken with salt and black pepper, and brown on all sides for 6 minutes in total.

3. Put in a plate. In a bowl, stir the onion soup mix with chicken broth and white wine, and add to the saucepan.

4. Simmer for 3 minutes and add the mushrooms and chicken.

5. Cover and simmer for another 20 minutes.

6. Stir in heavy cream and cook on low heat for 3 minutes.

7. Garnish with parsley to serve.

Nutritional Information: Calories 432, Total Fat 35.3g, Carbs 3.2g, Protein 24.2g

Mediterranean Chicken

Preparation time: 30 minutes

Serves: 2-4

Ingredients

- 2 tbsps. olive oil
- 1 onion, chopped
- 4 chicken breasts, skinless and boneless
- 4 garlic cloves, minced
- Salt and black pepper, to taste
- ½ cup Kalamata olives, pitted and chopped
- 1 tbsp. capers
- 1 tbsp. oregano
- ¼ cup white wine
- 1 cup tomatoes, chopped
- ½ tsp red chili flakes

Directions

1. Brush the chicken with half of the olive oil and sprinkle with black pepper and salt.

2. Heat a pan over high heat and cook the chicken for 2 minutes, flip to the other side, and cook for 2 more minutes.

3. Transfer to a baking dish, add in the white wine and 2 tbsps. of water. Bake in the oven at 380 F for 10-15 minutes.

4. Remove to a serving plate.

5. In the same pan, warm the remaining oil over medium heat.

6. Place in the onion, olives, capers, garlic, oregano, and chili flakes, and cook for 1 minute. Stir in the tomatoes, black pepper and salt, and cook for 2 minutes.

7. Sprinkle the sauce over the chicken breasts and serve.

Nutritional Information: Calories 365, Total Fat 22g, Carbs 3.1g, Protein 22.5g

Chicken Wings with Lemon Jalapeno Peppers

Preparation time: 65 minutes

Serves: 2-4

Ingredients

- 2 pounds' chicken wings
- Salt and black pepper, to taste
- 1 lemon, zested and juiced
- 3 tbsps. coconut aminos
- 3 tbsps. xylitol
- ¼ cup chives, chopped
- ½ tsp xanthan gum
- 5 dried jalapeño peppers, chopped

Directions

1. Preheat oven to 380 F and line a baking sheet with parchment paper.

2. Season the chicken with salt and black pepper and spread on the baking dish.

3. Bake for 35 minutes, and remove to a serving plate.

4. Put a small pan over medium heat, add in the lemon juice, coconut aminos, lemon zest, xylitol, xanthan gum, and jalapeño peppers.

5. Bring the mixture to a boil and cook for 2 minutes.

6. Pour the sauce over the chicken, sprinkle with chives and serve.

Nutritional Information: Calories 422, Total Fat 26.3g, Carbs 3.4g, Protein

*The Complete
Keto For Two Beginners Cookbook*

25.5g

Cheese and Bacon Stuffed Chicken

Preparation time: 30 minutes

Serves: 2

Ingredients

- 2 chicken fillets, skinless and boneless
- 1/2 teaspoon oregano
- 1/2 teaspoon tarragon
- 1/2 teaspoon paprika
- 1/4 teaspoon ground black pepper
- Sea salt, to taste
- 2 (1-ounce) slices bacon
- 2 (1-ounce) slices cheddar cheese
- 1 tomato, sliced

Directions

1. Sprinkle the chicken fillets with oregano, tarragon, paprika, black pepper, and salt.

2. Place the bacon slices and cheese on each chicken fillet. Roll up the fillets and secure with toothpicks.

3. Place the stuffed chicken fillets on a lightly greased baking pan.

4. Scatter the sliced tomato around the fillets.

5. Bake in the preheated oven at 390 degrees F for 15 minutes; turn on the other side and bake an additional 5 to 10 minutes or until the meat is no longer pink.

6. Discard the toothpicks and serve immediately.

Nutritional Information: Calories 401, Total Fat 23.9g, Carbs 3.7g, Protein 1.2g

Grilled Turkey Drumsticks

Preparation time: 20 minutes + Marinating time

Serves: 2

Ingredients

- 1 turkey drumstick, skinless and boneless
- 1 tablespoon balsamic vinegar
- 1 tablespoon whiskey
- 3 tablespoons olive oil
- 1 tablespoon stone ground mustard
- 1/2 teaspoon tarragon
- 1 teaspoon rosemary
- 1 teaspoon sage
- 1 garlic clove, pressed
- Kosher salt and ground black pepper, to season
- 1 brown onion, peeled and chopped

Directions

1. Place the turkey drumsticks in a ceramic dish. Toss them with the balsamic vinegar, whiskey, olive oil, mustard, tarragon, rosemary, sage, and garlic.

2. Cover with plastic wrap and refrigerate for 3 hours.

3. Heat your grill to the hottest setting.

4. Grill the turkey drumsticks for about 13 minutes per side.

5. Season with salt and pepper to taste and serve with brown onion.

Nutritional Information: Calories 388, Total Fat 19.5g, Carbs 6g, Protein 42g

Chicken Salad

Preparation time: 20 minutes

Serves: 2

Ingredients

- 2 chicken thighs, skinless
- Sea salt and cayenne pepper, to season
- 1/2 teaspoon Dijon mustard
- 1 tablespoon red wine vinegar
- 1/4 cup mayonnaise
- 1 small-sized celery stalk, chopped
- 2 spring onion stalks, chopped
- 1/2 head Romaine lettuce, torn into pieces
- 1/2 cucumber, sliced

Directions

1. Fry the chicken thighs until thoroughly heated and crunchy on the outside; an instant-read thermometer should read about 165 degrees F.

2. Discard the bones and chop the meat.

3. Place the other ingredients in a serving bowl and stir until everything is well incorporated.

4. Layer the chopped chicken thighs over the salad.

5. Serve well chilled and enjoy!

The Complete
Keto For Two Beginners Cookbook

Nutritional Information: Calories 456, Total Fat 29g, Carbs 6.7g, Protein 40.1g

Italian Chicken Meatballs

Preparation time: 15 minutes

Serves: 2

Ingredients

- ½ cup passata tomato sauce
- 1-pound ground chicken
- 2 tbsps. sun-dried tomatoes, chopped
- 2 tbsps. basil, chopped
- ½ tsp garlic powder
- 1 egg Salt and black pepper to taste
- ¼ cup almond flour
- 2 tbsps. olive oil
- ½ cup Parmesan cheese, shredded

Directions

1. To make meatballs, place everything except the oil and basil in a bowl. Mix with your hands until combined.
2. Form meatballs out of the mixture. Heat the olive oil in a skillet over medium heat.
3. Cook the meatballs for 3 minutes per each side.
4. To finish, pour over the tomato sauce and cook for 3-4 minutes.
5. Serve with sprinkled basil.

Nutritional Information: Calories 323, Total Fat 25.2g, Carbs 4.1g, Protein 21.5g

Eggplant & Carrot Chicken Gratin

Preparation time: 55 minutes

Serves: 2

Ingredients

- 2 tbsps. butter
- 1 tbsp. olive oil
- 1 eggplant, chopped
- 2 carrots, chopped
- 2 tbsps. Swiss cheese, grated
- Salt and black pepper, to taste
- 2 garlic cloves, minced
- 1-pound chicken thighs

Directions

1. Season the chicken with salt and pepper.

2. Put a pan over medium heat and warm 1 tbsp. butter with olive oil.

3. Place in the chicken thighs and cook each side for 3 minutes; lay them in a baking dish.

4. In the same pan, melt the rest of the butter and cook the garlic, eggplant, carrots, black pepper, and salt, for 10 minutes.

5. Top the chicken with this mixture and spread the cheese all over.

6. Bake in the oven at 350 F, for 30 minutes.

The Complete
Keto For Two Beginners Cookbook

Nutritional Information: Calories 405, Total Fat 31g, Carbs 6.6g, Protein 23g

Greek-Style Chicken Melange

Preparation time: 35 minutes

Serves: 2

Ingredients

- 2 ounces bacon, diced
- 3/4 pound whole chicken, boneless and chopped
- 1/2 medium-sized leek, chopped
- 1 teaspoon ginger garlic paste
- 1 teaspoon poultry seasoning mix
- Sea salt, to taste
- 1 bay leaf
- 1 thyme sprig
- 1 rosemary sprig
- 1 cup chicken broth
- 1/2 cup cauliflower, chopped into small florets
- 2 vine-ripe tomatoes, pureed

Directions

1. Heat a medium-sized pan over medium-high heat; once hot, fry the bacon until it is crisp or about 3 minutes.

2. Add in the chicken and cook until it is no longer pink; reserve. Then, sauté the leek until tender and fragrant.

3. Stir in the ginger garlic paste, poultry seasoning mix, salt, bay leaf, thyme, and rosemary.

4. Pour in the chicken broth and reduce the heat to medium; let it cook for 15 minutes, stirring periodically.

5. Add in the cauliflower and tomatoes along with the reserved bacon and chicken.

6. Decrease the temperature to simmer and let it cook for a further 15 minutes or until warmed through.

Nutritional Information: Calories 352, Total Fat 14.3g, Carbs 5.9g, Protein 44.2g

Sunday Chicken Bake

Preparation time: 30 minutes

Serves: 2

Ingredients

- 1 tablespoon olive oil
- 3/4-pound chicken breast fillets, chopped into bite-sized chunks
- 2 garlic cloves, sliced
- 1/4 teaspoon Korean chili pepper flakes
- 1/4 teaspoon Himalayan salt
- 1/2 teaspoon poultry seasoning mix
- 1 bell pepper, deveined and chopped
- 2 ripe tomatoes, chopped
- 1/4 cup heavy whipping cream
- 1/4 cup sour cream

Directions

1. Brush a casserole dish with olive oil. Add the chicken, garlic, Korean chili pepper flakes, salt, and poultry seasoning mix to the casserole dish.
2. Next, layer the pepper and tomatoes.
3. Whisk the heavy whipping cream and sour cream in a mixing bowl.
4. Top everything with the cream mixture.

5. Bake in the preheated oven at 390 degrees F for about 25 minutes or until thoroughly heated.

Nutritional Information: Calories 410, Total Fat 20.7g, Carbs 6.2g, Protein 50g

Feta & Bacon Chicken

Preparation time: 30 minutes

Serves: 2-4

Ingredients

- 4 oz. bacon, chopped
- 1-pound chicken breasts
- 3 green onions, chopped
- 2 tbsps. coconut oil
- 4 oz. feta cheese, crumbled
- 1 tbsp. parsley

Directions

1. Place a pan over medium heat and coat with cooking spray.

2. Add in the bacon and cook until crispy.

3. Remove to paper towels, drain the grease and crumble. To the same pan, add in the oil and cook the chicken breasts for 4-5 minutes, then flip to the other side; cook for an additional 4-5 minutes.

4. Add the chicken breasts to a baking dish.

5. Place the green onions, set in the oven, turn on the broiler, and cook for 5 minutes at high temperature.

6. Remove to serving plates and serve topped with bacon, feta cheese, and parsley.

The Complete
Keto For Two Beginners Cookbook

Nutritional Information: Calories 459, Total Fat 35g, Carbs 3.1g, Protein 31.5g

Baked Cheese Chicken Tenders

Preparation time: 34 minutes

Serves: 2-4

Ingredients

- 3 tbsps. olive oil
- 2 eggs, whisked
- 3 cups coarsely crushed cheddar cheese
- ½ cup pork rinds, crushed
- 1 lb. chicken tenders
- Salt to taste
- Lemon wedges for garnish

Directions

1. Preheat oven to 370 F and line a baking sheet with parchment paper.

2. Combine the eggs with the butter in a bowl, and mix the cheese and pork rinds in another bowl.

3. Season chicken with salt, dip in egg mixture, and coat generously in cheddar mixture. Place on the baking sheet, cover with aluminum foil and bake for 25 minutes.

4. Remove foil and bake further for 12 minutes to golden brown.

5. Serve chicken with lemon wedges.

Nutritional Information: Calories 512, Total Fat 43g, Carbs 2.2g, Protein 33.5g

Sauced Chicken Legs with Vegetables

Preparation time: 60 minutes

Serves: 2-4

Ingredients

- 2 tbsps. olive oil
- 1 parsnip, chopped
- 2 celery stalks, chopped
- 2 cups chicken stock
- 1 onion, chopped
- ¼ cup red wine
- 1-pound chicken legs
- 1 cup tomatoes, chopped
- 1 cup spinach
- ¼ tsp dried thyme
- Salt and black pepper, to taste
- 1 tbsp. parsley, chopped

Directions

1. Put a pot over medium heat and heat the olive oil.

2. Add garlic, parsnip, celery, and onion; season with salt and pepper and sauté for 5-6 minutes until tender.

3. Stir in the chicken and cook for 5 minutes.

4. Pour in the stock, tomatoes, and thyme, and cook for 30 minutes.

5. Sprinkle with parsley to serve.

Nutritional Information: Calories 264, Total Fat 14.5g, Carbs 7.1g, Protein 22.5g

Rosemary Chicken with Avocado Sauce

Preparation time: 22 minutes

Serves: 2

Ingredients

Sauce

- ¼ cup mayonnaise
- 1 avocado, pitted
- 1 tbsp. lemon juice
- Salt to taste

Chicken

- 2 tbsps. olive oil
- 2 chicken breasts
- Salt and black pepper to taste
- ½ cup rosemary, chopped
- ¼ cup warm water

Directions

1. Mash the avocado with a fork, in a bowl, and add in mayonnaise and lemon juice.

2. Warm olive oil in a large skillet, season the chicken with salt and black pepper and fry for 4 minutes on each side to golden brown.

3. Remove the chicken to a plate. Pour the warm water in the same skillet and add the rosemary.

4. Bring to simmer for 3 minutes and add the chicken.

5. Cover and cook on low heat for 5 minutes until the liquid has reduced and chicken is fragrant.

6. Dish chicken into serving plates and spoon the avocado sauce over.

Nutritional Information: Calories 406, Total Fat 34.1g, Carbs 3.9g, Protein 22.3g

Sage Chicken with Kale & Mushrooms

Preparation time: 40 minutes

Serves: 2

Ingredients

- 1-pound chicken thighs
- 2 cups mushrooms, sliced
- 1 cup kale, chopped
- 2 tbsps. butter
- 1 tbsp. olive oil
- Salt and black pepper, to taste
- ½ tsp onion powder
- ½ tsp garlic powder
- ½ cup water
- 1 tsp Dijon mustard
- 1 tbsp. fresh sage, chopped

Directions

1. Heat a pan over medium heat and warm half of the butter and olive oil.

2. Coat the chicken with onion powder, pepper, garlic powder and salt. Cook in the pan on each side for 3 minutes and set aside.

3. Stir in the remaining butter and mushrooms and cook for 5 minutes.

4. Place in water and mustard, take the chicken pieces back to the pan, and cook for 15 minutes. Stir in the kale and cook for 5 minutes.

5. Serve sprinkled with sage.

Nutritional Information: Calories 422, Total Fat 24.5g, Carbs 4.1g, Protein 27g

Paprika Chicken

Preparation time: 35 minutes

Serves: 4

Ingredients

- 4 (4-ounce) chicken breasts, skin-on
- Sea salt
- Freshly ground black pepper
- 1 tablespoon olive oil
- ½ cup chopped sweet onion
- ½ cup heavy (whipping) cream
- 2 teaspoons smoked paprika
- ½ cup sour cream
- 2 tablespoons chopped fresh parsley

Directions

1. Lightly season the chicken with salt and pepper.

2. Place a large skillet over medium-high heat and add the olive oil.

3. Sear the chicken on both sides until almost cooked through, about 15 minutes in total. Remove the chicken to a plate.

4. Add the onion to the skillet and sauté until tender, about 4 minutes.

5. Stir in the cream and paprika and bring the liquid to a simmer.

6. Return the chicken and any accumulated juices to the skillet and simmer the chicken for 5 minutes until completely cooked.

7. Stir in the sour cream and remove the skillet from the heat.

8. Serve topped with the parsley.

Nutritional Information: Calories 389, Total Fat 30g, Carbs 4g, Protein 25g

Carrot & Mushroom Chicken Skillet

Preparation time: 35 minutes

Serves: 2-4

Ingredients

- 1 cup carrots, shredded
- 1 cup mushrooms, sliced
- ½ tsp onion powder
- ½ tsp garlic powder
- 1 tbsp. butter
- 1 tbsp. olive oil
- ½ tsp Dijon mustard
- 1 tbsp. rosemary, chopped
- 1-pound chicken thighs
- Salt and black pepper, to taste

Directions

1. In a small bowl, mix together salt, black pepper, garlic, and onion powder.

2. Rub the chicken with the spice mixture. Warm the butter with olive oil in a skillet, and cook the chicken until browned, about 8-10 minutes; set aside.

3. Add mushrooms and carrots to the same fat and cook for about 5 minutes.

4. Season to taste with salt and black pepper. Stir in mustard and ¼ cup of water.

5. Return the chicken to the skillet and reduce the heat.

6. Cover and let simmer for 15 minutes. Scatter rosemary all over to serve.

Nutritional Information: Calories 452, Total Fat 36.5g, Carbs 3.2g, Protein 29g

Cabbage & Broccoli Chicken Casserole

Preparation time: 55 minutes

Serves: 2-4

Ingredients

- 1 tbsp. coconut oil, melted
- 2 cups mozzarella cheese, grated
- ½ head cabbage, shredded
- ½ head broccoli, cut into florets
- 1-pound chicken breasts, cooked and cubed
- 1 cup mayonnaise
- 1/3 cup chicken stock
- Salt and black pepper, to taste
- Juice of 1 lemon
- 1 tbsp. cilantro, chopped

Directions

1. Coat a baking dish with coconut oil and set chicken pieces to the bottom.

2. Spread green cabbage and broccoli, followed by half of the cheese.

3. In a bowl, combine the mayonnaise with black pepper, stock, lemon juice, and salt.

4. Pour this mixture over the chicken, spread the rest of the cheese, cover with aluminum foil, and bake for 30 minutes in the oven at 350 F.

5. Open the aluminum foil and cook for 20 more minutes. Sprinkle with cilantro to serve.

Nutritional Information: Calories 623, Total Fat 42g, Carbs 7.4g, Protein 51.5g

Lemon Butter Chicken

Preparation time: 50 minutes

Serves: 2-4

Ingredients

1. 4 bone-in, skin-on chicken thighs
2. Sea salt
3. Freshly ground black pepper
4. 2 tablespoons butter, divided
5. 2 teaspoons minced garlic
6. ½ cup Herbed Chicken Stock
7. ½ cup heavy (whipping) cream
8. Juice of ½ lemon

Directions

1. Preheat the oven to 400°F.
2. Lightly season the chicken thighs with salt and pepper.
3. Place a large ovenproof skillet over medium-high heat and add 1 tablespoon of butter.
4. Brown the chicken thighs until golden on both sides, about 6 minutes in total. Remove the thighs to a plate and set aside.
5. Add the remaining 1 tablespoon of butter and sauté the garlic until translucent, about 2 minutes.
6. Whisk in the chicken stock, heavy cream, and lemon juice.

7. Bring the sauce to a boil and then return the chicken to the skillet. 8. Place the skillet in the oven, covered, and braise until the chicken is cooked through, about 30 minutes.

Nutritional Information: Calories 294, Total Fat 26g, Carbs 4g, Protein 12g

Chapter Six: Sea Foods

Fish Jambalaya

Preparation time: 15 minutes

Serves: 2-4

Ingredients

- 1 teaspoon canola oil
- 1 jalapeno pepper, minced
- 1 small-sized leek, chopped
- 1/2 teaspoon ginger garlic paste
- 1/4 teaspoon ground cumin
- 1/4 teaspoon ground allspice
- 1/2 teaspoon oregano
- 1/4 teaspoon thyme
- 1/4 teaspoon marjoram
- 1-pound sole fish fillets, cut into bite-sized strips
- 1 large-sized ripe tomato, pureed
- 1/2 cup water
- 1/2 cup clam juice
- Kosher salt, to season
- 1 bay laurel

- 5-6 black peppercorns

- 1 cup spinach, torn into pieces

Directions

1. Heat the oil in a Dutch oven over a moderate flame.

2. Then, sauté the pepper and leek until they have softened.

3. Now, stir in the ginger-garlic paste, cumin, allspice, oregano, thyme, and marjoram; continue stirring for 30 to 40 seconds more or until aromatic.

4. Add in the fish, tomatoes, water, clam juice, salt, bay laurel, and black peppercorns.

5. Cover and decrease the temperature to medium-low. Let it simmer for 4 to 6 minutes or until the liquid has reduced slightly.

6. Stir in the spinach and let it simmer, covered, for about 2 minutes more or until it wilts. Ladle into serving bowls and serve warm.

Nutritional Information: Calories 232, Total Fat 6.7g, Carbs 3.6g, Protein 38.1g

Greek Sea Bass with Olive Sauce

Preparation time: 15 minutes

Serves: 2

Ingredients

- 2 sea bass fillets
- 2 tbsps. olive oil
- 1 garlic clove, minced
- A pinch of chili pepper
- 1 tbsp. green olives, pitted and sliced
- 1 lemon, juiced
- Salt to taste

Directions

1. Preheat a grill. In a small bowl mix together half of the olive oil, chili pepper, garlic, and salt and rub onto the sea bass fillets.

2. Grill the fish on both sides for 5-6 minutes until brown.

3. In a skillet over medium heat, warm the remaining olive oil and stir in the lemon juice, olives, and some salt; cook for 3-4 minutes. Plate the fillets and pour the lemon sauce over to serve.

Nutritional Information: Calories 267, Total Fat 15.6g, Carbs 1.6g, Protein 24g

Sardines with Green Pasta & Sun-Dried Tomatoes

Preparation time: 20 minutes

Serves: 2

Ingredients

- 2 tbsps. olive oil
- 4 cups zoodles (spiralled zucchini)
- ½ pound whole fresh sardines, gutted and cleaned
- ½ cup sun-dried tomatoes, drained and chopped
- 1 tbsps. dill
- 1 garlic clove, minced

Directions

1. Preheat the oven to 350 F and line a baking sheet with parchment paper.

2. Arrange the sardines on the dish, drizzle with olive oil, sprinkle with salt and black pepper. Bake in the oven for 10 minutes until the skin is crispy.

3. Warm oil in a skillet over medium heat and stir-fry the zucchini, garlic and tomatoes for 5 minutes.

4. Adjust the seasoning.

5. Transfer the sardines to a plate and serve with the veggie pasta.

Nutritional Information: Calories 232, Total Fat 6.7g, Carbs 3.6g, Protein 38.1g

Saucy Cod with Mustard Greens

Preparation time: 20 minutes

Serves: 2

Ingredients

- 1 tablespoon olive oil
- 1 bell pepper, seeded and sliced
- 1 jalapeno pepper, seeded and sliced
- 2 stalks green onions, sliced
- 1 stalk green garlic, sliced
- 1/2 cup fish broth
- 2 cod fish fillets
- 1/2 teaspoon paprika
- Sea salt and ground black pepper, to season
- 1 cup mustard greens, torn into bite-sized pieces

Directions

1. Heat the olive oil in a Dutch pot over a moderate flame.

2. Now, sauté the peppers, green onions, and garlic until just tender and aromatic.

3. Add in the broth, fish fillets, paprika, salt, black pepper, and mustard greens.

4. Reduce the temperature to medium-low, cover, and let it cook for 11 to 13 minutes or until heated through.

5. Serve immediately garnished with lemon slices if desired.

Nutritional Information: Calories 171, Total Fat 7.8g, Carbs 4.8g, Protein 20.3g

Baked Cod with Parmesan & Almonds

Preparation time: 40 minutes

Serves: 2

Ingredients

- 2 cod fillets
- 1 cup Brussels sprouts
- 1 tbsps. butter, melted
- Salt and black pepper to taste
- 1 cup crème fraiche
- 2 tbsps. Parmesan cheese, grated
- 2 tbsps. shaved almonds

Directions

1. Toss the fish fillets and Brussels sprouts in butter and season with salt and black pepper to taste.

2. Spread in a greased baking dish.

3. Mix the crème fraiche with Parmesan cheese, pour and smear the cream on the fish.

4. Bake in the oven for 25 minutes at 400 F until golden brown on top, take the dish out, sprinkle with the almonds and bake for another 5 minutes. Best served hot.

Nutritional Information: Calories 560, Total Fat 44.7g, Carbs 5.4g, Protein 25.3g

Fish Tacos with Slaw, Lemon and Cilantro

Preparation time: 20 minutes

Serves: 2

Ingredients

- 1 tbsp. olive oil
- 1 tsp chili powder
- 2 halibut fillets, skinless, sliced
- 2 low carb tortillas

Slaw

- 2 tbsps. red cabbage, shredded
- 1 tbsp. lemon juice
- Salt to taste
- ½ tbsp. extra-virgin olive oil
- ½ carrot, shredded
- 1 tbsp. cilantro, chopped

Directions

1. Combine red cabbage with salt in a bowl; massage cabbage to tenderize.
2. Add in the remaining slaw ingredient, toss to coat and set aside.
3. Rub the halibut with olive oil, chili powder and paprika.
4. Heat a grill pan over medium heat.

5. Add halibut and cook until lightly charred and cooked through, about 3 minutes per side. Divide between the tortillas.

6. Combine all slaw ingredients in a bowl. Split the slaw among the tortillas.

Nutritional Information: Calories 385, Total Fat 26g, Carbs 6.5g, Protein 23.8g

Fried Oysters in The Oven

Serves: 2-4

Preparation time: 20 minutes

Ingredients

- 3 tablespoons olive oil
- 1 teaspoon garlic salt
- 1 teaspoon freshly ground black pepper
- 1 teaspoon red pepper flakes
- 2 cups finely crushed pork rinds
- 24 shucked oysters

Directions

1. Preheat the oven to 400°F.

2. In a small bowl, mix together the olive oil, garlic salt, black pepper, and red pepper flakes.

3. Put the crushed pork rinds in a separate bowl.

4. Dip each oyster first in the oil mixture to coat and then in the pork rinds, turning to coat. Arrange the coated oysters on a baking sheet in a single layer with room in between.

5. Bake in the preheated oven for 30 minutes, or until the pork rind "breading" is browned and crisp. Serve hot.

Nutritional Information: Calories: 230, Carbs: 5g, Fat: 17g, Fiber: 0g, Protein: 15g

Tuna with Greens and Blueberries (One Pot)

Serves: 2

Preparation time: 10 minutes

Cooking time: 5 minutes

Ingredients

- ¼ cup olive
- 2 (4-ounce) tuna steaks
- Salt
- Freshly ground black pepper
- Juice of 1 lemon
- 4 cups salad greens
- ¼ cup low-carb, diary-free ranch dressing (Tessemae's)
- 20 blueberries

Directions

1. In a large skillet, heat the olive oil over medium-high heat.

2. Season the tuna steaks generously with salt and pepper, and add them to the skillet. Cook for 2 or 2 ½ minutes in each side to sear the outer edges.

3. Squeeze the lemon over the tuna in the pan and remove the fish

4. To serve, arrange the greens on 2 serving plates. Top each plate with one of the tuna steaks, 2 tablespoons of the ranch dressing, and 10 of the blueberries.

Nutritional Information: Calories: 549, Carbs: 7g, Fat: 41g, Fiber: 3g, Protein: 38g

Clarion Ulreich

Roasted Old Bay Prawns

Preparation time: 20 minutes

Serves: 2

Ingredients

- 3/4 pound prawns, peeled and deveined
- 1 teaspoon Old Bay seasoning mix
- 1/2 teaspoon paprika
- Coarse sea salt and ground black pepper, to taste
- 1 habanero pepper, deveined and minced
- 1 bell pepper, deveined and minced
- 1 cup pound broccoli florets
- 2 teaspoons olive oil
- 1 tablespoon fresh chives, chopped
- 2 slices lemon, for garnish
- 2 dollops of sour cream, for garnish

Directions

1. Toss the prawns with the Old Bay seasoning mix, paprika, salt, and black pepper. Arrange them on a parchment-lined roasting pan.

2. Add the bell pepper and broccoli.

3. Drizzle olive oil over everything and transfer the pan to a preheated oven.

4. Roast at 390 degrees F for 8 to 11 minutes, turning the pan halfway through the cooking time.

5. Bake until the prawns are pink and cooked through.

6. Serve with fresh chives, lemon, and sour cream.

Nutritional Information: Calories 269, Total Fat 9.6g, Carbs 7.2g, Protein 38.2g

Three-Minute Lobster Tail

Serves: 2

Preparation time: 5 minutes

Cooking time: 5 minutes

Ingredients

- 4 cups bone broth (or water)
- 2 lobster tails

Directions

1. In a large pot, bring the broth to a boil.

2. While the broth is coming to a boil, use kitchen shears to cut the back side of the lobster shell from end to end.

3. Place the lobster in the boiling broth and bring it back to a boil. Cook the lobster for 3 minutes.

4. Drain and serve immediately.

Nutritional Information: Calories: 154, Carbs: 0g, Fat: 2g, Fiber: 0g, Protein: 32g

Clarion Ulreich

Crispy Salmon with Broccoli & Red Bell Pepper

Preparation time: 30 minutes

Serves: 2

Ingredients

- 2 salmon fillets
- Salt and black pepper to taste
- 2 tbsps. mayonnaise
- 2 tbsps. fennel seeds, crushed
- ½ head broccoli, cut in florets
- 1 red bell pepper, sliced
- 1 tbsp. olive oil
- 2 lemon wedges

Directions

1. Brush the salmon with mayonnaise and season with salt and black pepper.

2. Coat with fennel seeds, place in a lined baking dish and bake for 15 minutes at 370 F.

3. Steam the broccoli and carrot for 3-4 minutes, or until tender, in a pot over medium heat. Heat the olive oil in a saucepan and sauté the red bell pepper for 5 minutes.

4. Stir in the broccoli and turn off the heat. Let the pan sit on the warm burner for 2-3 minutes.

5. Serve with baked salmon garnished with lemon wedges.

Nutritional Information: Calories 563, Total Fat 37g, Carbs 6g, Protein 38.2g

Easy Baked Halibut Steaks

Preparation time: 20 minutes

Serves: 2

Ingredients

- 2 tablespoons olive oil
- 2 halibut steaks
- 1 red bell pepper, sliced
- 1 yellow onion, sliced
- 1 teaspoon garlic, smashed
- 1/2 teaspoon hot paprika
- Sea salt cracked black pepper, to your liking
- 1 dried thyme sprig, leaves crushed

Directions

1. Start by preheating your oven to 390 degrees F.

2. Then, drizzle olive oil over the halibut steaks.

3. Place the halibut in a baking dish that is previously greased with a nonstick spray.

4. Top with the bell pepper, onion, and garlic.

5. Sprinkle hot paprika, salt, black pepper, and dried thyme over everything.

6. Bake in the preheated oven for 13 to 15 minutes and serve immediately. Enjoy!

Nutritional Information: Calories 502, Total Fat 19.1g, Carbs 5.7g, Protein 72g

Mediterranean Tilapia Bake

Preparation time: 30 minutes

Serves: 2

Ingredients

- 2 tilapia fillets
- 2 garlic cloves, minced
- 1 tsp basil, chopped
- 1 cup canned tomatoes
- ¼ tbsp. chili powder
- 2 tbsps. white wine
- 1 tbsp. olive oil
- ½ red onion, chopped
- 2 tbsps. parsley
- 10 black olives, pitted and halved

Directions

1. Preheat oven to 350 F. Heat the olive oil in a skillet over medium heat and cook the onion and garlic for about 3 minutes.

2. Stir in tomatoes, olives, chilli powder, and white wine and bring the mixture to a boil. Reduce the heat and simmer for 5 minutes.

3. Put the tilapia in a baking dish, pour over the sauce and bake in the oven for 10-15 minutes.

4. Serve garnished with basil.

Clarion Ulreich

Nutritional Information: Calories 282, Total Fat 15g, Carbs 6g, Protein 23g

Omelet Wraps with Tuna

Preparation time: 15 minutes

Serves: 2

Ingredients

- 1 avocado, sliced
- 1 tbsp. chopped chives
- 1/3 cup canned tuna, drained
- 2 spring onions, sliced
- 4 eggs, beaten
- 4 tbsps. mascarpone cheese
- 1 tbsp. butter
- Salt and black pepper, to taste

Directions

1. In a small bowl, combine the chives and mascarpone cheese; set aside.

2. Melt the butter in a pan over medium heat.

3. Add the eggs to the pan and cook for about 3 minutes. Flip the omelet over and continue cooking for another 2 minutes until golden.

4. Season with salt and black pepper. Remove the omelet to a plate and spread the chive mixture over. Arrange the tuna, avocado, and onion slices.

5. Wrap the omelet and serve immediately.

Nutritional Information: Calories 481, Total Fat 37.9g, Carbs 6.2g, Protein 26.9g

Baked Trout and Asparagus Foil Packets

Preparation time: 20 minutes

Serves: 2

Ingredients

- ½ pound asparagus spears
- 1 tbsp. garlic puree
- ½ pound deboned trout, butterflied
- Salt and black pepper to taste
- 3 tbsps. olive oil
- 2 sprigs rosemary
- 2 sprigs thyme
- 2 tbsps. butter
- ½ medium red onion, sliced
- 2 lemon slices

Directions

1. Preheat the oven to 400 F. Rub the trout with garlic puree, salt and black pepper. Prepare two aluminum foil squares.

2. Place the fish on each square.

3. Divide the asparagus and onion between the squares, top with a pinch of salt and pepper, a sprig of rosemary and thyme, and 1 tbsp. of butter.

4. Also, lay the lemon slices on the fish. Wrap and close the fish packets securely, and place them on a baking sheet.

5. Bake in the oven for 15 minutes, and remove once ready.

Nutritional Information: Calories 498, Total Fat 39.3g, Carbs 4.8g, Protein 27g

Coconut Shrimp

Serves: 2-4

Preparation time: 20 minutes

Cooking time: 30 minutes

Ingredients

- Avocado oil spray (or other cooking oil spray)
- 3 large egg whites
- 1 teaspoon cayenne
- 1 teaspoon garlic salt
- 1 teaspoon freshly ground black pepper
- ½ teaspoon Swerve granular (or another granulated alternative sweetener)
- 1 cup unsweetened shredded coconut
- 24 (or so) raw shrimp, peeled

Directions

1. Preheat the oven to 350°F. Spray a large baking sheet with the avocado oil spray.

2. In a small bowl, whisk together the egg whites, cayenne, garlic salt, pepper, and sweetener.

3. Put the shredded coconut in a separate bowl.

4. One at a time, dunk the shrimp first in the egg mixture and then in the coconut, turning to coat completely.

5. Arrange the coated shrimp on the prepared baking sheet in a single layer, with room in between. Once all the shrimp have been coated, spray them lightly with avocado oil spray.

6. Bake in the preheated oven for 30 minutes, or until the coconut is golden brown.

Nutritional Information: Calories: 223, Carbs: 7g, Fat: 17g, Fiber: 4g, Protein: 13g

Bacon-Wrapped Scallop Cups (One Pot)

Serves: 2-4

Preparation time: 10 minutes

Cooking time: 25 minutes

Ingredients

- 12 large sea scallops
- 6 strips bacon, halved to make 12 short strips
- 24 garlic cloves, peeled but left whole
- 5 tablespoons Lemon-Garlic Dressing

Directions

1. Preheat the oven to 400°F.

2. Wrap each scallop with 1 piece of bacon. Use a toothpick to secure the bacon to the scallop. Arrange the wrapped scallops on a baking sheet.

3. Place 2 garlic cloves on top of each scallop, then top with a spoonful of the dressing. 4Bake for 25 minutes, or until the bacon is browned and crisp.

Nutritional Information: Calories: 374, Carbs: 9g, Fat: 26g, Fiber: 4g, Protein: 26g

Sea Bass with Vegetables and Dill Sauce

Preparation time: 25 minutes

Serves: 2

Ingredients

- 1 tablespoon olive oil
- 1 cup red onions, sliced
- 2 bell peppers, deveined and sliced
- Sea salt and cayenne pepper, to taste
- 1 teaspoon paprika
- 1-pound sea bass fillets

Dill Sauce:

- 1 tablespoon mayonnaise
- 1/4 cup Greek yogurt
- 1 tablespoon fresh dill, chopped
- 1/2 teaspoon garlic powder
- 1/2 fresh lemon, juiced

Directions

1. Toss the onions, peppers, and sea bass fillets with the olive oil, salt, cayenne pepper, and paprika. Line a baking pan with a piece of parchment paper.

2. Preheat your oven to 400 degrees F.

3. Arrange your fish and vegetables on the prepared baking pan.

4. Bake for 10 minutes; turn them over and bake for a further 10 to 12 minutes.

5. Meanwhile, make the sauce by mixing all ingredients until well combined.

6. Serve the fish and vegetables with the dill sauce on the side.

Nutritional Information: Calories 374, Total Fat 17g, Carbs 6.2g, Protein 43.2g

Grilled Tuna Steaks with Shirataki Pad Thai

Preparation time: 30 minutes

Serves: 2

Ingredients

- ½ pack (7-oz) shirataki noodles
- 2 cups water
- 1 red bell pepper, seeded and sliced
- 2 tbsps. soy sauce, sugar-free
- 1 tbsp. ginger-garlic paste
- 1 tsp chili powder
- 1 tbsp. water
- 2 tuna steaks
- Salt and black pepper to taste
- 1 tbsp. olive oil
- 1 tbsp. parsley, chopped

Directions

1. In a colander, rinse the shirataki noodles with running cold water.

2. Bring a pot of salted water to a boil; blanch the noodles for 2 minutes.

3. Drain and set aside. Preheat a grill on medium-high.

4. Season the tuna with salt and black pepper, brush with olive oil, and grill covered.

5. Cook for 3 minutes on each side.

6. In a bowl, whisk together soy sauce, ginger-garlic paste, olive oil, chili powder, and water.

7. Add bell pepper, and dry noodles and toss to coat.

8. Assemble the noodles and tuna in serving plate and garnish with parsley.

Nutritional Information: Calories 287, Total Fat 16.2g, Carbs 6.8g, Protein 23.4g

Country Club Crab Cakes

Serves: 2-4

Preparation time: 30 minutes

Cooking time: 20 minutes

Ingredients

- 2 (6-ounce) cans crabmeat (or 12 ounces cooked crabmeat)
- 2 large eggs
- 2 tablespoons chopped fresh dill
- 1 teaspoon garlic salt
- ¼ cup olive oil

Directions

1. In a medium bowl, combine the crabmeat, eggs, dill, and garlic salt. Form the mixture into four patties.

2. In a medium skillet, heat the olive oil over medium heat. Cook the crab cakes for 3 to 4 minutes on each side, or until golden brown.

Nutritional Information: Calories: 212, Carbs: 1g, Fat: 16g, Protein: 16g

Coconut Fried Shrimp with Cilantro Sauce

Serves: 2

Preparation time: 15 minutes

Ingredients

- 2 tsp coconut flour
- 2 tbsps. grated Pecorino cheese
- 1 egg, beaten in a bowl
- ¼ tsp curry powder
- ½ pound shrimp, shelled
- 3 tbsps. coconut oil
- Salt to taste

Sauce

- 2 tbsps. ghee
- 2 tbsps. cilantro leaves, chopped
- ½ onion, diced
- ½ cup coconut cream
- ½ ounce Paneer cheese, grated

Directions

1. Combine coconut flour, Pecorino cheese, curry powder, and salt in a bowl.
2. Melt the coconut oil in a skillet over medium heat.
3. Dip the shrimp in the egg first, and then coat with the dry mixture.

4. Fry until golden and crispy, about 5 minutes. In another skillet, melt the ghee.

5. Add onion and cook for 3 minutes. Add curry and cilantro and cook for 30 seconds.

6. Stir in coconut cream and Paneer cheese and cook until thickened.

7. Add the shrimp and coat well. Serve warm.

Nutritional Information: Calories: 741, Carbs: 4.3g, Fat: 64g, Protein: 34.4g

Shrimp Sti-fry

Serves: 2

Preparation time: 10 minutes

Cooking time: 20 minutes

Ingredients

- ¼ cup avocado oil
- ¼ cup coconut aminos
- 2 cups chopped broccoli
- 1 onion, diced
- 1 red bell pepper, chopped
- 24 cooked and peeled shrimp
- 1 (12-ounce) bag riced cauliflower
- Chili sauce, for serving (Optional)

Directions

1. Combine the shrimp, Cauliflower, onion, pepper, broccoli, coconut aminos, and avocado oil in a large skillet. Cook, stirring occasionally, until all the flavors are combined, about 20 minutes

2. Drizzle the chili sauce over the top and serve hot

Nutritional Information: Calories: 231, Carbs: 12g, Fat: 15g, Fiber: 5g, Protein: 12g

Baked Salmon with Lemon and Mush

Serves: 2

Preparation time: 10 minutes

Cooking time: 30 minutes

Ingredients

- 2 (6-ounce) skin-on salmon fillets
- 1 onion, diced
- 8 ounces' mushrooms, sliced
- ¼ cup olive oil
- 1 teaspoon salt
- 1 teaspoon freshly ground black pepper
- 4 lemon slices

Directions

1. Preheat the oven to 400°F.

2. Tear off 2 large squares of aluminum foil. Place a salmon fillet on each piece of foil and arrange the onion and mushrooms over and around the fish, dividing evenly.

3. Pour the olive oil over the fish, then season with the salt and pepper. Top each piece of fish with 2 lemon slices.

4. Wrap the foil up around the salmon and vegetables, leaving room inside the packet for heat to circulate, and bake for 30 minutes, or until the fish flakes easily with a fork. Serve hot.

Nutritional Information: Calories: 576, Carbs: 8g, Fat: 44g, Fiber: 3g, **Protein:** 37g

Pan-fried Soft Shell Crab

Serves: 2

Preparation time: 5 minutes

Cooking time: 10 minutes

Ingredients

- ½ cup olive oil
- ½ cup almond flour
- 1 teaspoon paprika
- 1 teaspoon garlic salt
- 1 teaspoon freshly ground black pepper
- 2 soft-shell crabs

Directions

1. Fill the bottom of a heavy skillet with the oil and heat over low heat.

2. While the oil is heating, in a medium bowl, mix together the almond flour, paprika, garlic salt, and pepper.

3. Dredge each crab in the flour mixture, coating both sides and shaking off any excess. Put the crabs into the hot oil in the skillet and cook for about 5 minutes per side, or until golden brown.

4. Serve hot.

Nutritional Information: Calories: 489, Carbs: 6g, Fat: 33g, Fiber: 2g, Protein: 42g

Chilli Cod with Chive Sauce

Serves: 2

Preparation time: 20 minutes

Ingredients

- 1 tsp chilli powder
- 2 cod fillets
- Salt and black pepper to taste
- 1 tbsp olive oil
- 1 garlic clove, minced
- 1/3 cup lemon juice
- 2 tbsps. vegetable stock
- 2 tbsps. chives, chopped

Directions

1. Preheat oven to 400 F and grease a baking dish with cooking spray.

2. Rub the cod fillets with chili powder, salt, and black pepper and lay in the baking dish.

3. Bake for 10-15 minutes until fish fillets are easily removed with a fork.

4. In a skillet over low heat, warm the olive oil and sauté the garlic for 3 minutes.

5. Add the lemon juice, vegetable stock, and chives.

6. Season with salt, black pepper, and cook for 3 minutes until the stock slightly reduces.

7. Divide fish into 2 plates, top with sauce, and serve.

Nutritional Information: Calories: 448, Carbs: 6.3g, Fat: 35.3g, Protein: 42g

Pan-Seared Scallops with Sausage & Mozzarella

Serves: 2-4 minutes

Preparation time: 15 minutes

Ingredients

- 2 tbsps. butter
- 12 fresh scallops, rinsed and pat dry
- 8 ounces sausage, chopped
- 1 red bell pepper, seeds removed, sliced
- 1 red onion, finely chopped
- 1 cup Grana Padano cheese, grated
- Salt and black pepper to taste

Directions

1. Melt half of the butter in a skillet over medium heat, and cook the onion and bell pepper for 5 minutes until tender.

2. Add the sausage and stir-fry for another 5 minutes.

3. Remove and set aside. Pat dry the scallops with paper towels, and season with salt and pepper.

4. Add the remaining butter to the skillet and sear the scallops for 2 minutes on each side to have a golden brown color.

5. Add the sausage mixture back, and warm through.

6. Transfer to serving platter and top with Grana Padano cheese.

The Complete
Keto For Two Beginners Cookbook

Nutritional Information: Calories: 834, Carbs: 9.5g, Fat: 62g, Protein: 56g

Chapter Seven: Beef & Pork Recipes

Secret Seasoning Sirloin Steak

Serves: 2

Preparation time: 25 minutes

Ingredients

- 2 (6- to 8-ounce) sirloin steaks, at room temperature
- ¼ cup sugar-free ketchup (such as Primal Kitchen)
- 4 teaspoons garlic salt
- ¼ cup olive oil

Directions

1. Heat the broiler to high.

2. Lay out the steaks on a plate and cover each side with the ketchup and garlic salt.

3. In a cast iron skillet, heat the oil over high heat. Add the steaks and cook for 1 minute on each side.

4. Transfer the skillet to the broiler and cook for 5 minutes more.

5. Remove the skillet from the oven, flip the steaks over, and let them continue to cook in the hot pan for 10 more minutes.

6. Serve immediately.

Nutritional Information: Calories 462, Carbs: 3g, Fat: 34g, Fiber: 2g, Protein: 36g

Slopy Joes

Serves: 2

Preparation time: 40 minutes

Ingredients

- 1-pound ground beef
- 1 onion, diced
- ¾ cup sugar-free ketchup (such as Primal Kitchen)
- 2 tablespoons garlic powder
- 1 tablespoon white vinegar
- 1 tablespoon
- Swerve granular (or another granulated alternative sweetener)

Directions

1. Heat a large skillet over medium-high heat. Add the meat and cook, stirring, until it begins to brown, about 3 minutes. Add the onion and cook, stirring frequently, until the meat is browned, and the onion is softened, about 5 minutes.

2. Stir in the ketchup, garlic powder, vinegar, and sweetener. Reduce the heat to medium-low and cook for 20 minutes more. Serve hot.

Nutritional Information: Calories 356, Carbs: 4g, Fat: 28g, Fiber: 1g, Protein: 19g

Fajita Kabobs

Serves: 2-4

Preparation time: 16 minutes

Ingredients

- ¼ cup lime juice
- ¼ avocado oil
- 2 cloves garlic, minced
- 1 teaspoon fine sea salt
- ¾ cayenne pepper
- 1 teaspoon chili powder
- ½ teaspoon paprika
- ½ teaspoon ground cumin
- 2 (8-ounce) boneless rib-eye steaks, about 1 inch thick
- 8 grape tomatoes
- 1 red onion
- 2 green bell peppers
- ½ cup Citrus Avocado salsa, for serving
- Boston lettuce leaves, for serving

Directions

1. Make the marinade: Place the oil, lime juice, garlic, salt, and spices in a large bowl

2. Cut the steaks into 1-inch cubes. Add the meat to marinade and stir to coat well. Cover and refrigerate for at least 1 hour or overnight

3. Preheat a grill to high heat. While the grill is heating up, cut the bell peppers and onion into 1-inch squares. Remove the meat from the marinade; reserve the marinade for basting.

4. Place 2 cubes of steak on a skewer, followed by an onion piece, a steak piece, a bell pepper piece, a steak piece, and a grape tomato, then repeat the sequence with another piece of steak, then onion, steak, and bell pepper, ending with 2 pieces of steak. Repeat with the remaining skewers and ingredients.

5. Lightly brush the hot grill grates with oil. Place the skewers on the grill for 3 minutes, basting every minute with the reserved marinade. Flip and cook, basting, for another 3 minutes for medium-rare steak.

6. Serve with salsa and lettuce leaves for wrapping, if desired

7. Store in an airtight container in the refrigerator for up to 4 days. To reheat, place in a skillet over medium heat, stirring often, for a few minutes, until warmed to your liking.

Nutritional Information: Calories 370, Carbs: 10g, Fat: 28g, Fiber: 2g, Protein: 21g

Mini Meatloaves with Spinach

Serves: 2-4

Preparation time: 35 minutes

Ingredients

- 1/2-pound lean ground beef
- 2 tablespoons tomato paste
- 1 teaspoon Dijon mustard
- 1 egg, beaten
- 1/2 teaspoon ginger garlic paste
- 1/2 cup shallots, finely chopped
- 1 tablespoon canola oil
- 1/2 teaspoon coconut aminos
- 1/4 cup almond meal
- 1 bunch spinach, chopped
- 1 teaspoon dried parsley flakes
- 1/2 teaspoon dried basil
- 1/2 teaspoon dried rosemary
- 1/2 teaspoon dried sage
- 1/4 teaspoon cayenne pepper
- Kosher salt and ground black pepper
- 2 tablespoons sour cream

Directions

1. Mix all of the above ingredients, except for the sour cream, until everything is well incorporated.

2. Press the meat mixture into a lightly greased muffin tin.

3. Bake the mini meatloaves in the preheated oven at 360 degrees F for 20 to 28 minutes.

4. Serve with sour cream and enjoy!

Nutritional Information: Calories 434, Carbs: 4.4g, Fat: 29.4g, Protein: 37.1g

Cabbage Slaw with Ground Beef (One Pot)

Serves: 2-4

Preparation time: 35 minutes

Ingredients

- 3 tablespoons olive oil
- 1-pound ground beef
- 1 (16-ounce) bag cabbage slaw mix
- 3 tablespoons coconut aminos
- 1 tablespoon fish sauce (such as Red Boat)

Directions

1. Heat the olive oil in a large skillet over medium-high heat. Add the meat and cook, stirring, until browned, about 7 minutes. Add the cabbage and cook, stirring occasionally, until wilted, about 15 minutes.

2. Stir in the coconut aminos and fish sauce, and simmer for 5 minutes more.

3. Serve hot or cover and store in the refrigerator for up to 5 days.

Nutritional Information: Calories 463, Carbs: 10g, Fat: 39g, Fiber: 1g, Protein: 18g

Sticky Barbecued Ribs

Serves: 2-4

Preparation time: 1 hour 35 minutes

Ingredients

- 1 tablespoon olive oil
- 1/2-pound beef ribs
- 1 leek, sliced
- 1/4 cup red wine
- 1/2 cup vegetable broth
- 1/2 teaspoon cumin powder
- 1/2 teaspoon ginger powder
- Kosher salt and cayenne pepper, to taste
- 1 teaspoon liquid smoke
- 1 teaspoon granulated garlic
- 1/4 teaspoon stevia powder
- 1 teaspoon American-style mustard
- 1 tablespoon sesame seeds, toasted
- 2 tablespoons fresh chives, chopped

Directions

1. Heat the olive oil in a pan over a moderate flame.

2. Now, sear the beef ribs for 3 to 4 minutes on each side; stir in the leek and cook an additional 3 minutes.

3. Add a splash of wine to deglaze the pan. Now, add in the remaining wine, broth, cumin powder, ginger powder, salt, and pepper.

4. Decrease the temperature to medium-low, cover, and let it cook for 40 minutes. Now, line a baking dish with foil.

5. Place the ribs along with the cooking liquid in the baking dish.

6. Add in the liquid smoke, garlic, stevia, and American-style mustard.

7. Bake in the preheated oven at 300 degrees F for 1 hour; make sure to turn the ribs periodically to ensure they are coated with the glaze. Top with sesame seeds and chives.

Nutritional Information: Calories 481, Carbs: 5.9g, Fat: 41g, Fiber: 1.3g, Protein: 19.9g

Kielbasa and Sauerkraut (One Pot)

Serves: 2-4

Preparation time: 15 minutes

Ingredients

- 1 (16-ounce) jar or can sauerkraut
- 1-pound pork kielbasa, diced
- 2 tablespoons olive oil

Directions

1. In a medium saucepan, bring the sauerkraut to a boil over medium-high heat. Add the diced sausage and the olive oil, and simmer over low heat until heated through, about 5 minutes.

Nutritional Information: Calories 435, Carbs: 6g, Fat: 39g, Fiber: 3g, Protein: 29g

Rich and Easy Pork Ragout

Serves: 2

Preparation time: 40 minutes

Ingredients

- 1 teaspoon lard, melted at room temperature
- 3/4-pound pork butt, cut into bite-sized cubes
- 1 red bell pepper, deveined and chopped
- 1 poblano pepper, deveined and chopped
- 2 cloves garlic, pressed
- 1/2 cup leeks, chopped
- Sea salt and ground black pepper, to season
- 1/2 teaspoon mustard seeds
- 1/4 teaspoon ground allspice
- 1/4 teaspoon celery seeds
- 1 cup roasted vegetable broth
- 2 vine-ripe tomatoes, pureed

Directions

2. Melt the lard in a stockpot over moderate heat.

3. Once hot, cook the pork cubes for 4 to 6 minutes, stirring occasionally to ensure even cooking.

4. Then, stir in the vegetables and continue cooking until they are tender and fragrant.

5. Add in the salt, black pepper, mustard seeds, allspice, celery seeds, roasted vegetable broth, and tomatoes. Reduce the heat to simmer.

6. Let it simmer for 30 minutes longer or until everything is heated through. Ladle into individual bowls and serve hot.

Nutritional Information: Calories 497, Carbs: 35.3g, Fat: 2.5g, Fiber: 3g, Protein: 0.6g

Mexican Style Beef Casserole

Serves: 2-4

Preparation time: 55 minutes

Ingredients

- 1 tablespoon canola oil
- 1/2-pound blade steak, sliced into strips
- 1 bell pepper, seeded and chopped
- 1 jalapeno pepper, seeded and chopped
- 1 cup cauliflower florets
- 1 medium-sized leek, thinly sliced
- 1/2 teaspoon Mexican oregano
- 1 teaspoon paprika
- 1 vine-ripe tomato, pureed
- 2 tablespoons apple cider vinegar
- 1/2 cup roasted vegetable broth
- 3/4 cup Manchego cheese, shredded

Directions

1. Heat the canola oil in a Dutch oven over medium-high flame.

2. Now, cook the beef for 5 to 6 minutes, stirring periodically to ensure even cooking.

3. Now, stir in the peppers, cauliflower, and leeks; continue cooking an additional 4 minutes or until the vegetables are tender and aromatic.

4. Add in the Mexican oregano, paprika, tomatoes, vinegar and broth.

5. Decrease the temperature to simmer and let it cook for a further 30 minutes.

6. Spoon the mixture into a casserole dish; top with the Manchego and bake for 10 to 13 minutes or until the cheese has melted and the edges are bubbling.

7. Let it rest for 10 minutes before cutting and serving. Enjoy!

Nutritional Information: Calories 452, Carbs: 7.1g, Fat: 32.1g, Fiber: 2.1g, Protein: 29.2g

Pork Loin Steaks in Creamy Pepper Sauce

Serves: 2

Preparation time: 15 minutes

Ingredients

- 1 teaspoon lard, at room temperature
- 2 pork loin steaks
- 1/2 cup beef bone broth
- 2 bell peppers, deseeded and chopped
- 1 shallot, chopped
- 1 garlic clove, minced
- Sea salt, to season
- 1/2 teaspoon cayenne pepper
- 1/4 teaspoon paprika
- 1 teaspoon Italian seasoning mix
- 1/4 cup Greek-style yogurt

Directions

1. Melt the lard in a cast-iron skillet over moderate heat.

2. Once hot, cook the pork loin steaks until slightly browned or approximately 5 minutes per side; reserve.

3. Add a splash of the beef bone broth to deglaze the pan.

4. Now, cook the bell peppers, shallot, and garlic until tender and aromatic.

5. Season with salt, cayenne pepper, paprika, and Italian seasoning mix.

6. After that, decrease the temperature to medium-low, add the

7. Greek yogurt to the skillet and let it simmer for 2 minutes more or until heated through.

8. Serve immediately.

Nutritional Information: Calories 447, Carbs: 6g, Fat: 19.2g, Fiber: 1.3g, Protein: 62.2g

Pork Medallions with Cabbage

Serves: 2

Preparation time: 15 minutes

Ingredients

- 1-ounce bacon, diced
- 2 pork medallions
- 2 garlic cloves, sliced
- 1 red onion, chopped
- 1 jalapeno pepper, deseeded and chopped
- 1 tablespoon apple cider vinegar
- 1/2 cup chicken bone broth
- 1/3-pound red cabbage, shredded
- 1 bay leaf
- 1 sprig rosemary
- 1 sprig thyme
- Kosher salt and ground black pepper, to taste

Directions

1. Heat a Dutch pot over medium-high heat. Once hot, cook the bacon until it is crisp or about 3 minutes; reserve.

2. Now, cook the pork medallions in the bacon grease until they are browned on both sides.

3. Add the remaining ingredients and reduce the heat to medium-low. Let it cook for 13 minutes more, gently stirring periodically to ensure even cooking.

4. Taste and adjust the seasonings. Serve in individual bowls topped with the reserved fried bacon.

Nutritional Information: Calories 528, Carbs: 31.8g, Fat: 6.3g, Protein: 51.2g

Sticky Barbecued Ribs

Serves: 2-4

Preparation time: 1 hr. 45 minutes

Ingredients

- 1 tablespoon olive oil
- 1/2-pound beef ribs
- 1 leek, sliced
- 1/4 cup red wine
- 1/2 cup vegetable broth
- 1/2 teaspoon cumin powder
- 1/2 teaspoon ginger powder
- Kosher salt and cayenne pepper, to taste
- 1 teaspoon liquid smoke
- 1 teaspoon granulated garlic
- 1/4 teaspoon stevia powder '
- 1 teaspoon American-style mustard
- 1 tablespoon sesame seeds, toasted
- 2 tablespoons fresh chives, chopped

Directions

1. Heat the olive oil in a pan over a moderate flame. Now, sear the beef ribs for 3 to 4 minutes on each side; stir in the leek and cook an additional 3 minutes.

2. Add a splash of wine to deglaze the pan.

3. Now, add in the remaining wine, broth, cumin powder, ginger powder, salt, and pepper. Decrease the temperature to medium-low, cover, and let it cook for 40 minutes. Now, line a baking dish with foil.

4. Place the ribs along with the cooking liquid in the baking dish.

5. Add in the liquid smoke, garlic, stevia, and American-style mustard.

6. Bake in the preheated oven at 300 degrees F for 1 hour; make sure to turn the ribs periodically to ensure they are coated with the glaze. Top with sesame seeds and chives.

Nutritional Information: Calories 452, Carbs: 32.1g, Fat: 32.1g, Fiber: 7.1g, Protein: 39.2g

Mom's Festive Meatloaf

Serves: 2-4

Preparation time: 1 hour

Ingredients

- 1/4-pound ground pork
- 1/2-pound ground chuck
- 2 eggs, beaten
- 1/4 cup flaxseed meal
- 1 shallot, chopped
- 2 garlic cloves, minced
- 1/4 teaspoon ground black pepper, or more to taste
- 1/2 teaspoon smoked paprika
- 1/4 teaspoon dried basil
- 1/4 teaspoon ground cumin Kosher salt, to taste
- 1/2 cup tomato puree
- 1 teaspoon mustard
- 1 teaspoon liquid monk fruit

Directions

7. In a mixing bowl, thoroughly combine the ground meat, eggs, flaxseed meal, shallot, garlic, and spices.

8. In another bowl, mix the tomato puree with the mustard and liquid monk fruit; whisk to combine well. Press the mixture into the loaf pan.

9. Bake in the preheated oven at 360 degrees F for 30 minutes.

10. Spread the tomato mixture on top of the meatloaf.

11. Return to the oven and bake for 20 to 25 minutes more or until cooked through. Let it rest for 8 to 10 minutes before slicing.

12. Cut with a serrated bread knife and enjoy!

Nutritional Information: Calories 517, Carbs: 8.4g, Fat: 32.3g, Protein: 48g

Rich Winter Beef Stew

Serves: 2-4

Preparation time: 45 minutes

Ingredients

- 1-ounce bacon, diced
- 3/4-pound well-marbled beef chuck, boneless and cut into 1-1/2-inch pieces
- 1 red bell pepper, chopped
- 1 green bell pepper, chopped
- 2 garlic cloves, minced
- 1/2 cup leeks, chopped
- 1 parsnip, chopped
- Sea salt, to taste
- 1/4 teaspoon mixed peppercorns, freshly cracked
- 2 cups chicken bone broth
- 1 tomato, pureed
- 2 cups kale, torn into pieces
- 1 tablespoon fresh cilantro, roughly chopped

Directions

1. Heat a Dutch pot over medium-high flame. Now, cook the bacon until it is well browned and crisp; reserve.

2. Then, cook the beef pieces for 3 to 5 minutes or until just browned on all sides; reserve.

3. After that, sauté the peppers, garlic, leeks, and parsnip in the pan drippings until they are just tender and aromatic.

4. Add the salt, peppercorns, chicken bone broth, tomato, and reserved beef to the pot. Bring to a boil.

5. Turn the heat to simmer and let it cook for 25 to 35 minutes more or until everything is cooked through.

6. Lastly, stir in the kale leaves and continue simmering until the leaves have wilted or 3 to 4 minutes more.

7. Ladle into individual bowls and serve garnished with fresh cilantro and the reserved bacon.

Nutritional Information: Calories 359, Carbs: 5.4g, Fat: 17.8g, Protein: 43g

Beef and Garden Vegetable Soup

Serves: 2-4

Preparation time: 35 minutes

Ingredients

- 1 teaspoon olive oil
- 1/2-pound lean ground beef
- 1/2 cup celery stalks, chopped
- 1/2 cup scallions, chopped
- 1 jalapeno pepper, chopped
- 1 cup green cabbage, shredded
- 2 cups chicken bone broth
- 1/4 teaspoon cayenne pepper
- 1 teaspoon ground coriander
- 1/2 teaspoon ground bay leaf
- Kosher salt and freshly cracked black pepper, to taste
- 1 vine-ripe tomato, pureed
- 1 tablespoon apple cider vinegar

Directions

1. Heat the olive oil in a medium-sized stockpot over medium-high flame.
2. Now, brown the ground beef until no longer pink.

3. Stir in the celery, scallions, and jalapeno pepper; continue cooking an additional 3 minutes or until your vegetables have softened.

4. Then, stir in the remaining ingredients, cover, and decrease the temperature to medium-low.

5. Let it simmer for 30 minutes or until thoroughly heated.

Nutritional Information: Calories 299, Carbs: 6.5g, Fat: 15.1g, Protein: 32g

Chunky Pork Soup with Mustard Greens

Serves: 2

Preparation time: 25 minutes

Ingredients

- 1 tablespoon olive oil 1 bell pepper, deveined and chopped
- 2 garlic cloves, pressed
- 1/2 cup scallions, chopped
- 1/2-pound ground pork
- 1 cup beef bone broth
- 1 cup water
- 1/2 teaspoon crushed red pepper flakes
- Sea salt and freshly cracked black pepper, to season
- 1 bay laurel
- 1 teaspoon fish sauce
- 2 cups mustard greens, torn into pieces
- 1 tablespoon fresh parsley, chopped

Directions

1. Heat the olive oil in a stockpot over a moderate flame.

2. Coat, once hot, sauté the pepper, garlic, and scallions until tender or about 3 minutes.

3. After that, stir in the ground pork and cook for 5 minutes more or until well browned, stirring periodically.

4. Add in the beef bone broth, water, red pepper, salt, black pepper, and bay laurel. Reduce the temperature to simmer and cook, covered, for 10 minutes.

5. Afterwards, stir in the fish sauce and mustard greens.

6. Remove from the heat; let it stand until the greens are wilted. Ladle into individual bowls and serve garnished with fresh parsley.

Nutritional Information: Calories 344, Carbs: 6.3g, Fat: 25.2g, Protein: 23.1g

Asian Spiced Beef with Broccoli

Serves: 2

Preparation time: 30 minutes

Ingredients

- ½ cup coconut milk
- 2 tbsps. coconut oil
- ¼ tsp garlic powder
- ¼ tsp onion powder
- ½ tbsp. coconut aminos
- 1-pound beef steak, cut into strips
- Salt and black pepper, to taste
- 1 head broccoli, cut into florets
- ½ tbsps. Thai green curry paste
- 1 tsp ginger paste
- 1 tbsp. cilantro, chopped
- ½ tbsp. sesame seeds

Directions

1. Warm coconut oil in a pan over medium heat, add in the beef, season with garlic powder, black pepper, salt, ginger paste, and onion powder and cook for 4 minutes.

2. Mix in the broccoli and stir-fry for 5 minutes.

3. Pour in the coconut milk, coconut aminos, and Thai curry paste and cook for 15 minutes.

4. Serve sprinkled with cilantro and sesame seeds.

Nutritional Information: **Calories 623, Carbs: 2.3g, Fat: 43.2g, Protein: 53.5g**

Easy Spicy Meatballs

Serves: 2

Preparation time: 25 minutes

Ingredients

- 1-ounce bacon, diced
- 2 pork medallions
- 2 garlic cloves, sliced
- 1 red onion, chopped
- 1 jalapeno pepper, deseeded and chopped
- 1 tablespoon apple cider vinegar
- 1/2 cup chicken bone broth
- 1/3-pound red cabbage, shredded
- 1 bay leaf
- 1 sprig rosemary
- 1 sprig thyme
- Kosher salt and ground black pepper, to taste

Directions

1. Heat a Dutch pot over medium-high heat.

2. Once hot, cook the bacon until it is crisp or about 3 minutes; reserve.

3. Now, cook the pork medallions in the bacon grease until they are browned on both sides.

4. Add the remaining ingredients and reduce the heat to medium-low. Let it cook for 13 minutes more, gently stirring periodically to ensure even cooking. Taste and adjust the seasonings.

5. Serve in individual bowls topped with the reserved fried bacon.

Nutritional Information: Calories 528, Carbs: 51.2g, Fat: 6.3g, Protein: 51.2g

Easy Spicy Meatballs

Serves: 2

Preparation time: 25 minutes

Ingredients

- 1 tablespoon ground flax seeds
- 2 ounces' bacon rinds
- 1/2-pound ground pork
- 1 garlic clove, minced
- 1/2 cup scallions, chopped
- Sea salt and cayenne pepper, to taste
- 1/2 teaspoon smoked paprika
- 1/4 teaspoon ground cumin
- 1/4 teaspoon mustard seeds
- 1/2 teaspoon fennel seeds
- 1/2 teaspoon chili pepper flakes
- 2 tablespoons olive oil

Directions

1. In a mixing bowl, thoroughly combine all ingredients, except for the olive oil, until well combined. Form the mixture into balls and set aside.

2. Heat the olive oil in a nonstick skillet and fry the meatballs for about 15 minutes or until cooked through.

3. Serve with marinara sauce if desired.

Nutritional Information: Calories 557, Carbs: 50.1g, Fat: 2.3g, Protein: 0.5g

Veggie Beef Stew with Root Mash

Serves: 1 hr. 50 minutes

Preparation time: 2 minutes

Ingredients

- 1 tbsp. olive oil
- 1 parsnip, chopped
- 1 garlic clove, minced
- 1 onion, chopped
- 1 celery stalk, chopped
- ½ pound stewing beef, cut into chunks
- Salt and black pepper to taste
- 1 ¼ cups beef stock
- 2 bay leaves
- 1 carrot, chopped
- ½ tbsp. fresh rosemary, chopped
- 1 tomato, chopped
- 2 tbsps. red wine
- ½ cauliflower head, cut into florets
- ½ celeriac, chopped
- 2 tbsps. butter

Directions

1. In a pot, cook the celery, onion, and garlic, in warm oil over medium heat for 5 minutes. Stir in the beef chunks, and cook for 3 minutes.

2. Season with salt and black pepper. Deglaze the bottom of the pot by adding the red wine.

3. Add in the carrot, parsnip, beef stock, tomato, and bay leaves. Boil the mixture, reduce the heat to low and cook for 1 hour and 30 minutes.

4. Meanwhile, heat a pot with water over medium heat.

5. Place in the celeriac, cover and simmer for 10 minutes.

6. Add in the cauliflower florets, cook for 15 minutes, drain everything and combine with butter, pepper and salt.

7. Mash using a potato masher and split the mash between 2 plates.

8. Top with vegetable mixture and stewed beef, sprinkle with rosemary and serve.

Nutritional Information: Calories 465, Carbs: 9.8g, Fat: 24.5g, Protein: 32g

Pulled Pork with Mint and Cheese

Serves: 2

Preparation time: 20 minutes

Ingredients

- 1 teaspoon lard, melted at room temperature
- 3/4 pork Boston butt, sliced
- 2 garlic cloves, pressed
- 1/2 teaspoon red pepper flakes, crushed
- 1/2 teaspoon black peppercorns, freshly cracked
- Sea salt, to taste
- 2 bell peppers, deveined and sliced
- 1 tablespoon fresh mint leaves, snipped
- 4 tablespoons cream cheese

Directions

1. Melt the lard in a cast-iron skillet over a moderate flame.

2. Once hot, brown the pork for 2 minutes per side until caramelized and crispy on the edges.

3. Reduce the temperature to medium-low and continue cooking another 4 minutes, turning over periodically.

4. Shred the pork with two forks and return to the skillet.

5. Add the garlic, red pepper, black peppercorns, salt, and bell pepper and continue cooking for a further 2 minutes or until the peppers are just tender and fragrant.

6. Serve with fresh mint and a dollop of cream cheese. Enjoy!

Nutritional Information: Calories 370, Carbs: 21.9g, Fat: 5.1g, Protein: 34.9g

Roast Beef with Herbs

Serves: 2-4

Preparation time: 1hr 10 minutes

Ingredients

- 1-pound rump roast, boneless
- 1 tablespoon yellow mustard
- 1 teaspoon dried thyme
- 1/2 teaspoon dried rosemary
- 1 teaspoon dried parsley flakes
- Sea salt and freshly ground black pepper, to taste
- 1/2 cup beef bone broth
- 4 garlic cloves, peeled and halved
- 2 yellow onions, quartered

Directions

1. Pat the roast dry with paper towels. Then, rub the roast with the mustard and spices on all sides.

2. Place the rump roast in a roasting pan; pour in the beef broth.

3. Scatter the garlic and onions around the meat and transfer to the preheated oven.

4. Roast at 360 degrees F for 30 minutes. Then lower the heat to 220 degrees F and roast for 30 to 40 minutes more.

Nutritional Information: Calories 316, Carbs: 2.6g, Fat: 13.2g, Protein: 47.2g

Pork Cutlets with Spanish Onion

Serves: 2-4

Preparation time: 15 minutes

Ingredients

- 1 tablespoon olive oil
- 2 pork cutlets
- 1 bell pepper, deveined and sliced
- 1 Spanish onion, chopped
- 2 garlic cloves, minced
- 1/2 teaspoon hot sauce
- 1/2 teaspoon mustard
- 1/2 teaspoon paprika
- Coarse sea salt and ground black pepper, to taste

Directions

1. Heat the olive oil in a large saucepan over medium-high heat.

2. Then, fry the pork cutlets for 3 to 4 minutes until evenly golden and crispy on both sides.

3. Decrease the temperature to medium and add the bell pepper, Spanish onion, garlic, hot sauce, and mustard; continue cooking until the vegetables have softened, for a further 3 minutes.

4. Sprinkle with paprika, salt, and black pepper. Serve immediately and enjoy!

Nutritional Information: Calories 24.1, Carbs: 2.6g, Fat: 3.4g, Protein: 40.1g

Flank Steak Roll

Serves: 2

Preparation time: 42 minutes

Ingredients

- 1 lb. flank steak
- Salt and black pepper to taste
- ½ cup ricotta cheese, crumbled
- ½ cup baby kale, chopped
- 1 serrano pepper, chopped
- 1 tbsp. basil leaves, chopped

Directions

1. Wrap the steak in plastic wraps, place on a flat surface, and gently run a rolling pin over to flatten. Take off the wraps.

2. Sprinkle with half of the ricotta cheese, top with kale, serrano pepper, and the remaining cheese. Roll the steak over on the stuffing and secure with toothpicks.

3. Place in the greased baking sheet and cook for 30 minutes at 390 F, flipping once until nicely browned on the outside and the cheese melted within.

4. Cool for 3 minutes, slice and serve with basil.

Nutritional Information: Calories 445, Carbs: 2.8g, Fat: 21g, Protein: 53g

Grilled Steak with Herb Butter & Green Beans

Serves: 2

Preparation time: 20 minutes

Ingredients

- 2 ribeye steaks
- 2 tbsps. unsalted butter
- 1 tsp olive oil
- ½ cup green beans, sliced
- Salt and ground pepper, to taste
- 1 tbsp. fresh thyme, chopped
- 1 tbsp. fresh rosemary, chopped
- 1 tbsp. fresh parsley, chopped

Directions

1. Brush the steaks with olive oil and season with salt and black pepper.

2. Preheat a grill pan over high heat and cook the steaks for about 4 minutes per side; set aside.

3. Steam the green beans for 3-4 minutes until tender. Season with salt.

4. Melt the butter in the pan and stir-fry the herbs for 1 minute; then mix in the green beans.

5. Transfer over the steaks and serve.

Nutritional Information: Calories 576, Carbs: 4.3g, Fat: 39g, Protein: 51g

Beef Burgers with Iceberg Lettuce & Avocado

Serves: 2

Preparation time: 15 minutes

Ingredients

- ½ pound ground beef
- 1 green onion, chopped
- ½ tsp garlic powder
- 1 tbsp. butter
- Salt and black pepper to taste
- 1 tbsp. olive oil
- ½ tsp Dijon mustard
- 2 low carb buns, halved
- 2 tbsps. mayonnaise
- ½ tsp balsamic vinegar
- 2 tbsps. iceberg lettuce, chopped
- 1 avocado, sliced

Directions

1. In a bowl, mix together the beef, green onion, garlic powder, mustard, salt, and black pepper; create 2 burgers.

2. Heat the butter and olive oil in a skillet and cook the burgers for about 3 minutes per side.

3. Fill the buns with lettuce, mayonnaise, balsamic vinegar, burgers, and avocado slices to serve.

Nutritional Information: Calories 778, Carbs: 5.6g, Fat: 62g, Protein: 34g

Juicy Beef with Rosemary & Thyme

Serves: 2-4

Preparation time: 25 minutes

Ingredients

- 2 garlic cloves, minced
- 2 tbsps. butter
- 2 tbsps. olive oil
- 1 tbsp. fresh rosemary, chopped
- 1-pound beef rump steak, sliced
- Salt and black pepper, to taste
- 1 shallot, chopped
- ½ cup heavy cream
- ½ cup beef stock
- 1 tbsp. mustard
- 2 tsp soy sauce, sugar-free
- 2 tsp lemon juice
- 1 tsp xylitol
- A sprig of rosemary
- A sprig of thyme

Directions

1. Set a pan to medium heat, warm in a tbsp of olive oil and stir in the shallot; cook for 3 minutes.

2. Stir in the stock, soy sauce, xylitol, thyme sprig, cream, mustard and rosemary sprig, and cook for 8 minutes. Stir in butter, lemon juice, pepper and salt. Get rid of the rosemary and thyme. Set aside.

3. In a bowl, combine the remaining oil with black pepper, garlic, rosemary, and salt. Toss in the beef to coat, and set aside for some minutes.

4. Heat a pan over medium-high heat, place in the beef steak, cook for 6 minutes, flipping halfway through; set aside and keep warm.

5. Plate the beef slices, sprinkle over the sauce, and enjoy.

Nutritional Information: Calories 441, Carbs: 4.6g, Fat: 31g, Protein: 28.5g

Veggie Chuck Roast Beef in Oven

Serves: 2-4

Preparation time: 1 hr. 40 minutes

Ingredients

- 2 tbsps. olive oil
- 1-pound beef chuck roast, cubed
- 1 cup canned diced tomatoes
- 1 carrot, chopped
- Salt and black pepper, to taste
- ½ pound mushrooms, sliced
- 1 celery stalk, chopped
- 1 bell pepper, sliced
- 1 onion, chopped
- 1 bay leaf
- ½ cup beef stock
- 1 tbsp. fresh rosemary, chopped
- ½ tsp dry mustard
- 1 tbsp. almond flour

Directions

1. Preheat oven to 350 F. Set a pot over medium heat, warm olive oil and brown the beef on each side for 4-5 minutes.

2. Stir in tomatoes, onion, mustard, carrot, mushrooms, bell pepper, celery, and stock. Season with salt and pepper.

3. In a bowl, combine ½ cup of water with flour and stir in the pot.

4. Transfer to a baking dish and bake for 90 minutes, stirring at intervals of 30 minutes.

5. Scatter the rosemary over and serve warm.

Nutritional Information: Calories 325, Carbs: 5.6g, Fat: 17.8g, Protein: 31.5g

Chapter Eight: Soups, Stews & Salads

Chicken and Lime Soup

Serves: 2-4

Preparation time: 30mins

Ingredients

- 2 lbs. (500 g) chicken breast
- 8 oz. (250 g) mushrooms
- 4 1/4 c (1 liter) chicken broth
- 2 limes
- 1 chili pepper
- 1 bunch of green onions
- Oil
- Salt and pepper to season

Directions

1. Thinly slice the green onions, chili pepper and the mushrooms.

2. Cut the chicken breast into cubes and season with salt and pepper. Sauté the meat in a pot with a little oil until golden brown.

3. Add the chicken broth and boil briefly.

4. Meanwhile remove the ends from the limes and cut the rest into thick slices. Add these along with the mushrooms, Spanish onions and chilies to the hot broth

and simmer on low for about 15 minutes. The lime slices can be removed before serving, the taste will remain. However, the lime slices will look very nice in a bowl.

5. If desired, season with soy sauce, but this will slightly darken the clear broth.

Nutritional Information: Calories 182, Fats 5.1g, Carbs 4.6g, Protein 29.9g

Fennel Salad

Serves: 2-4

Preparation time: 20mins

Ingredients

- 2 bulbs of fennel
- 1 radicchio
- 1 lime
- 3/4 c (200 g) yogurt
- Olive oil
- Balsamic vinegar
- Salt and pepper to season

Directions

1. Wash the fennel and trim off the fronds and the stalk. Then thinly slice or shave the fennel. Always use the finger guard when using a cheese slicer, since the blades are often a lot sharper than they seem. Slightly pull the fennel apart and add to a salad bowl.

2. Wash the radicchio, spin dry in a salad spinner and cut into bite size pieces or strips. Add to the fennel and toss with salad servers.

3. For the dressing mix equal parts of vinegar and oil. Add to the yogurt. Then season to taste with salt and pepper and a little lime juice and pour over the salad. If you like limes, you can also grate the zest and sprinkle it over the salad.

Nutritional Information: Calories 196, Fats 11.4g, Carbs 6.9g, Protein 5.2g

Spicy Habanero Cheeseburger Soup

Preparation time: 20 minutes

Serves: 2

Ingredients

- 1/8 teaspoon garlic powder or to taste
- 2 tablespoons grated habanero cheddar or pepper jack
- 2 tablespoons grated extra sharp cheddar reserve one teaspoon
- 1 tablespoon butter
- 1 tablespoon finely chopped onion
- 1/4 cup cooked seasoned ground beef
- 1/4 cup heavy cream
- 1/2 cup water

Directions

1. Sauté the onion in the butter until soft and the onion just starts to turn golden
2. Add the heavy cream and the water and bring to a simmer
3. Simmer for 2 minutes to reduce slightly
4. Stir in all but the one teaspoon reserved cheese.
5. Stir until melted and smoothly mixed with the cream mixture
6. Add the cooked ground beef
7. Simmer for another 2 or 3 minutes so the flavors can blend
8. Spoon into a bowl and sprinkle reserved cheese on top

Nutritional Information: Calories 425, Carbs 2.3g, Total Fat 39.9g, Protein 14.8g

Green Chicken Enchilada Soup

Preparation time: 20 minutes

Serves: 2-4

Ingredients

- 1 cup sharp cheddar cheese, shredded
- 2 cups bone broth or chicken stock
- 2 cups cooked chicken, shredded
- 1/2 cup salsa Verde (see example)
- 4 oz. cream cheese, softened

Directions

1. In a blender, combine the salsa, cream cheese, cheddar cheese and chicken stock and blend until smooth.

2. Pour into a medium saucepan and cook on medium until hot – don't bring to a boil. Otherwise, you can heat this in a microwave safe bowl in 1 minute increments until hot. Stir in between each minute.

3. Add the shredded chicken and cook until heated through, about 5 minutes.

4. Garnish with additional shredded cheddar and chopped cilantro if desired.

Nutritional Information: Calories 346, Carbs 3g, Total Fat 22g, Protein 32g

Cream" of Broccoli Soup

Preparation time: 20 minutes

Serves: 2

Ingredients

- 1 Small Avocado
- ½ tsp Ground Nutmeg
- 2 cups bone broth
- 1-2 large "Heads" of Broccoli

Directions

1. Wash and cut broccoli into florets, then slice stems.

2. Peel and pit avocado. Cut into medium-size chunks.

3. In a medium sized pot over medium high heat, bring the bone broth to a simmer.

4. Add the broccoli and steam for about 8 minutes, until dark green and tender. Then reduce heat to low.

5. Add the nutmeg and avocado chunks to the pot. Continue to cook until avocado has warmed, about 3 to 4 minutes.

6. Puree with an Immersion Blender, or use a Blender or Food Processor, being careful not to burn yourself.

7. Serve!

Nutritional Information: Calories 346, Carbs 3g, Total Fat 22g, Protein 32g

Creamy Zucchini Soup

Preparation time: 30 minutes

Serves: 2-4

Ingredients

- 1 tablespoon butter, ghee or olive oil
- 1 tsp salt
- 3 cups chicken stock
- ¼ cup packed fresh basil leaves
- 2 lbs. zucchini, about 4-5, chopped, but leave peel on for color
- ¾ cup onion, chopped
- 2 garlic cloves, minced

Directions

1. In a soup pot over medium low heat, cook the onion and garlic in butter/ghee for about 3-5 minutes.

2. Add the zucchini and salt, turn the heat to medium and cook for an additional 5 minutes.

3. Add the chicken stock and simmer for 15 minutes. Stir in basil. Puree with an immersion blender.

4. Serve!

Easy Pumpkin Soup

Preparation time: 20 minutes

Serves: 2-4

Ingredients

- 1/2 tsp garlic powder
- 1 tsp fresh thyme
- 1/2 cup heavy cream
- 15 oz. pumpkin puree
- 4 cups chicken broth
- 1/2 tsp salt
- 1/2 tsp pepper
- 2 tbsps. chopped parsley

Directions

1. To a medium sauce pan, add the pumpkin puree, chicken broth, salt, pepper, garlic, and thyme. Stir to combine.

2. Bring the mixture to a boil, then reduce heat and simmer for about 10 minutes, to give the flavors time to meld.

3. Remove from the heat, and add the heavy cream.

4. Garnish with parsley and serve.

Nutritional Information: Calories 120, Carbs 9g, Total Fat 7g, Protein 2g

Spinach Salad with Goat Cheese & Pine Nuts

Preparation time: 20 minutes

Serves: 2

Ingredients

- 2 cups spinach
- ½ cup pine nuts
- 1 ½ cups hard goat cheese, grated
- 2 tbsps. white wine vinegar
- 2 tbsps. extra virgin olive oil
- Salt and black pepper, to taste

Directions

1. Preheat oven to 390 F. Place the grated goat cheese in two circles on two pieces of parchment paper.

2. Place in the oven and bake for 10 minutes. Find two same bowls, place them upside down, and carefully put the parchment paper on top to give the cheese a bowl-like shape.

3. Let cool that way for 15 minutes. Divide spinach among the bowls sprinkle with salt and pepper and drizzle with vinegar and olive oil.

4. Top with pine nuts to serve.

Nutritional Information: Calories 410, Carbs 3.4g, Total Fat 31.2g, Protein 27g

Pesto Caprese Salad with Tuna

Preparation time: 10 minutes

Serves: 2

Ingredients

- 1 tomato, sliced
- 4 oz. canned tuna chunks in water, drained
- 1 ball fresh mozzarella cheese, sliced
- 4 basil leaves
- ½ cup pine nuts
- ½ cup Parmesan cheese, grated
- ½ cup extra virgin olive oil
- ½ lemon, juiced

Directions

1. Put in a food processor the basil leaves, pine nuts, Parmesan cheese and extra virgin olive oil, and blend until smooth.

2. Add in the lemon juice. Arrange the cheese and tomato slices in a serving plate.

3. Scatter the tuna chunks and pesto over the top and serve.

Nutritional Information: Calories 364, Carbs 3.4g, Total Fat 31g, Protein 21g

Spinach Salad with Bacon & Mustard Vinaigrette

Preparation time: 20 minutes

Serves: 2

Ingredients

- 1 cup spinach
- 1 large avocado, sliced
- 1 spring onion, sliced
- 2 bacon slices
- ½ lettuce head, shredded
- 1 hard-boiled egg, chopped

Vinaigrette:

- Salt to taste
- ¼ tsp garlic powder
- 3 tbsps. olive oil
- 1 tsp Dijon mustard
- 1 tbsp. white wine vinegar

Directions

1. Chop the bacon and fry in a skillet over medium heat for 5 minutes until crispy.

2. Set aside to cool. Mix the spinach, lettuce, egg, and spring onion, in a bowl.

3. Whisk together the vinaigrette ingredients in another bowl.

4. Pour the dressing over, toss to combine and top with avocado and bacon.

Nutritional Information: Calories 547, Carbs 4.7g, Total Fat 51g, Protein 11.7g

Caesar Salad

Preparation time: 10 minutes

Serves: 2-4

Ingredients

- 1 avocado, pitted, peeled, and sliced
- Salt and ground black pepper, to taste
- 3 tablespoons creamy Caesar dressing
- 1 cup bacon, cooked and crumbled
- 1 chicken breast, grilled and shredded

Directions

1. In a salad bowl, mix the avocado with bacon and chicken breast, and stir.
2. Add the dressing, salt, and pepper, toss to coat, divide into 2 bowls, and serve.

Nutritional Information: Calories 334, Total Fats 23g, Carbs 3g, Protein 18g

Keto Egg Salad

Preparation time: 30 minutes

Serves: 2-4

Ingredients

- Splash of lemon juice (to prevent avocado browning)
- 1/8 Tsp Dill (If desired)
- 1/2 Tbsp. fresh chopped parsley (If desired)
- Salt and pepper, to taste
- 1 medium Avocado
- 6 Eggs
- 1/3 Cup Mayonnaise
- 1 Tsp Dijon Mustard

Directions

1. In a saucepan, cover the eggs with water in a saucepan. Bring to a boil, turn heat off, cover and rest in hot water for 10-15 minutes.

2. Peel shell (Run under cold water first)

3. slice the eggs into small pieces, sprinkle with salt and pepper and set aside

4. Mash avocado and sprinkle with salt and pepper

5. Mix mayo, eggs, mashed avocado, mustard, lemon juice and choice of herbs in a medium bowl

6. Chill and serve

The Complete
Keto For Two Beginners Cookbook

Nutritional Information: Calories 575, Total Fats 51g, Carbs 7g, Protein 20g

Classic Greek Salad

Preparation time: 10 minutes

Serves: 2-4

Ingredients

- 3 tbsps. extra virgin olive oil
- ½ lemon, juiced
- 3 tomatoes, sliced
- 1 cucumber, sliced
- 1 red bell pepper, sliced
- 1 small red onion, chopped
- 10 Kalamata olives, chopped
- 4 oz. feta cheese, cubed
- 1 tsp parsley, chopped
- Salt to taste

Directions

1. Mix the olive oil with lemon juice and salt, in a small bowl.

2. In a salad plate, combine the tomatoes, cucumber, bell pepper and parsley; toss with the dressing.

3. Top with the feta and olives, and serve.

Nutritional Information: Calories 223, Total Fats 21g, Carbs 1.9g, Protein 6.8g

Salad of Prawns and Mixed Lettuce Greens

Preparation time: 15 minutes

Serves: 2

Ingredients

- 2 cups mixed lettuce greens
- ¼ cup aioli
- 1 tbsp. olive oil
- ½ pound tiger prawns, peeled and deveined
- ½ tsp Dijon mustard
- Salt and chili pepper to season
- 1 tbsp. lemon juice

Directions

1. Season the prawns with salt and chili pepper. Fry in warm olive oil over medium heat for 3 minutes on each side until prawns are pink. Set aside.

2. Add the aioli, lemon juice and mustard in a small bowl. Mix until smooth and creamy.

3. Place the mixed lettuce greens in a bowl and pour half of the dressing on the salad.

4. Toss with 2 spoons until mixed, and add the remaining dressing.

5. Divide salad among plates and serve with prawns.

Nutritional Information: Calories 445, Total Fats 31.5g, Carbs 3.4g, Protein 31g

Pump up your Greens 'Creamed' Soup

Preparation time: 5 minutes

Serves: 2-4

Ingredients

- 1/4 cup gluten-free vegetable broth
- 1 clove garlic
- 1 tablespoon brags soy seasoning
- 1 tablespoon lemon juice
- pinch chili powder (optional)
- freshly ground pepper, to taste
- 2 cups spinach leaves
- 1 avocado
- 1/2 cup English cucumber
- 1 green onion
- 1/2 cup red bell pepper

Directions

Put all ingredients in the blender and blend until smooth.

Nutritional Information: Calories 95, Carbs 6.7g, Total Fat 7.6g, Protein 2.1g

Green Chicken Enchilada Soup

Preparation time: 20 minutes

Serves: 2-4

Ingredients

- 1 cup sharp cheddar cheese, shredded
- 2 cups bone broth or chicken stock
- 2 cups cooked chicken, shredded
- 1/2 cup salsa Verde (see example)
- 4 oz. cream cheese, softened

Directions

5. In a blender, combine the salsa, cream cheese, cheddar cheese and chicken stock and blend until smooth.

6. Pour into a medium saucepan and cook on medium until hot – don't bring to a boil. Otherwise, you can heat this in a microwave safe bowl in 1 minute increments until hot. Stir in between each minute.

7. Add the shredded chicken and cook until heated through, about 5 minutes.

8. Garnish with additional shredded cheddar and chopped cilantro if desired.

Nutritional Information: Calories 346, Carbs 3g, Total Fat 22g, Protein 32g

Spicy Habanero Cheeseburger Soup

Preparation time: 20 minutes

Serves: 2

Ingredients

- 1/8 teaspoon garlic powder or to taste
- 2 tablespoons grated habanero cheddar or pepper jack
- 2 tablespoons grated extra sharp cheddar reserve one teaspoon
- 1 tablespoon butter
- 1 tablespoon finely chopped onion
- 1/4 cup cooked seasoned ground beef
- 1/4 cup heavy cream
- 1/2 cup water

Directions

9. Sauté the onion in the butter until soft and the onion just starts to turn golden
10. Add the heavy cream and the water and bring to a simmer
11. Simmer for 2 minutes to reduce slightly
12. Stir in all but the one teaspoon reserved cheese.
13. Stir until melted and smoothly mixed with the cream mixture
14. Add the cooked ground beef
15. Simmer for another 2 or 3 minutes so the flavors can blend
16. Spoon into a bowl and sprinkle reserved cheese on top

Nutritional Information: Calories 425, Carbs 2.3g, Total Fat 39.9g, Protein 14.8g

Cream of Mushroom Soup

Preparation time: 30 minutes

Serves: 2

Ingredients

- 1/4 teaspoon Himalayan rock salt
- Freshly ground pepper, to taste
- 1/2 teaspoon extra-virgin olive oil
- 2 cups cauliflower florets
- 1 2/3 cup unsweetened original almond milk
- 1 teaspoon onion powder
- 1 1/2 cups diced white mushrooms
- 1/2 yellow onion, diced

Directions

1. In a small saucepan, place cauliflower, milk, onion powder, salt and pepper. Cover and bring to a boil over medium heat.

2. Turn down heat to low and simmer until cauliflower is softened, about 8 minutes. Then, puree using a food processor, or blender.

3. To a medium sized saucepan, add oil, mushrooms and onion to a medium-sized saucepan. Heat over high heat for about 8 minutes, until onions are translucent and beginning to brown.

4. Add pureed cauliflower mixture to sautéed mushrooms. Bring to a boil, cover and simmer for 10 minutes, until thickened.

5. Serve immediately.

Nutritional Information: Calories 425, Carbs 4g, Total Fat 7.9g, Protein 4.9g

Minty Green Chicken Salad

Preparation time: 25 minutes

Serves: 2

Ingredients

- 1 chicken breast, cubed
- 1 tbsp. avocado oil
- 2 eggs
- 2 cups green beans, steamed
- 1 avocado, sliced
- 4 cups mixed salad greens
- 2 tbsps. olive oil
- 2 tbsps. lemon juice
- 1 tsp Dijon mustard
- 1 tbsp. mint, chopped
- Salt and black pepper, to taste

Directions

1. Boil the eggs in salted water over medium heat for 10 minutes.
2. Remove to an ice bath to cool, peel and slice.
3. Warm the oil in a pan over medium heat. Add the chicken and cook for about 4 minutes.
4. Divide the green beans between two salad bowls.

5. Top with chicken, eggs, and avocado slices.

6. In another bowl, whisk together the lemon juice, olive oil, mustard, salt, and pepper, and drizzle over the salad.

7. Top with mint and serve.

Nutritional Information: Calories 612, Carbs 6.9g, Total Fat 47.9g, Protein 4.9g

Celery & Cauliflower Soup with Bacon Croutons

Preparation time: 25 minutes

Serves: 2

Ingredients

- 2 tbsps. olive oil
- 1 onion, chopped
- ¼ celery root, grated
- 1 head cauliflower, cut into florets
- 3 cups water
- Salt and black pepper to taste
- 1 cup almond milk
- 1 cup white cheddar cheese, shredded
- 2 oz. bacon, cut into strips

Directions

1. Sauté the onion in warm olive oil over medium heat for 3 minutes until fragrant. Include the cauli florets and celery root, sauté for 3 minutes to slightly soften, add the water, and season with salt and black pepper.

2. Bring to a boil, and then reduce the heat to low. Cover and cook for 10 minutes. Puree the soup with an immersion blender until the ingredients are evenly combined and stir in the almond milk and cheese until the cheese melts.

3. Adjust taste with salt and black pepper. In a non-stick skillet over high heat, fry the bacon, until crispy.

4. Divide soup between serving bowls, top with crispy bacon, and serve hot.

Nutritional Information: Calories 323, Carbs 7.6g, Total Fat 27g, Protein 22.8g

Avocado cucumber ginger salad recipe

Preparation time: 5 minutes

Serves: 2

Ingredients

- 1/2 cucumber, peeled and diced small
- 1/2 avocado, diced small
- 1 teaspoon lemon juice
- 1 Tablespoon sesame oil or olive oil [Use olive oil for AIP]
- Salt to taste
- 1 Tablespoon goji berries
- 1 Tablespoon freshly grated ginger

Nutritional Information: Calories 110, Carbs 1g, Total Fat 10g, Protein 6g

Shrimp and Arugula Salad

Preparation time: 10 minutes

Serves: 2-4

Ingredients

- 1 avocado diced
- 8 cups baby arugula
- 1-pound large cooked shrimp
- 4 tablespoons good quality extra virgin olive oil
- 2 lemons 1 juiced and 1 cut into wedges
- coarse sea salt and fresh cracked pepper

Directions

1. To a large bowl, add arugula, shrimp, and avocado. Drizzle with half of the olive oil, juice of one lemon, and salt and pepper to taste.

2. Toss lightly, then add more olive oil, if needed, to just lightly coat arugula. Taste and adjust seasonings.

3. Serve with lemon wedges on the side.

Nutritional Information: Calories 343, Total Fat 23g, Carbs 10g, Protein 25g

Keto cucumber salad

Preparation time: 5 minutes

Serves: 2

Ingredients

- 2 Tablespoons of lemon juice (30 ml)
- 1 cucumber (220 g), sliced and then quartered
- 2 Tablespoons of mayo (30 ml)
- Freshly ground black pepper and salt, to taste

Directions

1. In a small bowl, mix together the cucumber slices, mayo, and lemon juice. Add salt and pepper to taste.

Nutritional Information: Calories 116, Total Fat 12g, Carbs 2g, Protein 1g

Feta & Sun-Dried Tomato Salad with Bacon

Preparation time: 10 minutes

Serves: 2

Ingredients

- 3 oz. bacon slices, chopped
- 5 sun-dried tomatoes in oil, sliced
- 4 basil leaves
- 1 cup feta cheese, crumbled
- 2 tsp extra virgin olive oil
- 1 tsp balsamic vinegar
- Salt to taste

Directions

2. Fry the bacon in a pan over medium heat, until golden and crisp, for about 5 minutes. Remove with a perforated spoon and set aside.

3. Arrange the sun-dried tomatoes on a serving plate.

4. Scatter feta cheese over and top with basil leaves.

5. Add the crispy bacon on top, drizzle with olive oil and sprinkle with vinegar and salt.

Nutritional Information: Calories 411, Total Fat 36g, Carbs 2.5g, Protein 16.2g

Chinese Tofu Soup

Preparation time: 15 minutes

Serves: 2

Ingredients

- 2 cups chicken stock
- 1 tbsp. soy sauce, sugar-free
- 2 spring onions, sliced
- 1 tsp sesame oil, softened
- 2 eggs, beaten 1-inch piece ginger, grated
- Salt and black ground, to taste
- ½ pound extra-firm tofu, cubed
- A handful of fresh cilantro, chopped

Directions

1. Boil in a pan over medium heat, soy sauce, chicken stock and sesame oil.

2. Place in eggs as you whisk to incorporate completely.

3. Change heat to low and add salt, spring onions, black pepper and ginger; cook for 5 minutes. Place in tofu and simmer for 1 to 2 minutes.

4. Divide into soup bowls and serve sprinkled with fresh cilantro.

Nutritional Information: Calories 411, Total Fat 36g, Carbs 2.5g, Protein 16.2g

Chapter Ten: Vegan and Vegetarian Recipes

Almond Pancakes

Preparation time: 20 minutes

Serves: 2-4

Ingredients

- 2/3 c (100 g) ground almonds
- 1 c (100 g) protein powder
- 2 Tbs (25 g) Stevia
- 1 1/2 c (350 ml) milk
- 1 vanilla bean
- 5 tsp (1 pkg) baking powder
- Oil

Directions

1. In a bowl whisk the ground almonds, protein powder, sugar substitute, baking powder and the milk to a smooth batter. To prevent clumps, you can also use a hand mixer.

2. Cut the vanilla bean in half and scrape out the pulp with a knife.

3. Add to the batter and briefly blend again. Heat a pan with oil on the stove, use a ladle to pour pancakes into the hot pan and cook.

4. Cook the almond pancakes about 2-3 minutes each side until golden brown. The almond pancakes are great both warm and cold and you can easily use the different low carb spreads to vary them.

Nutritional Information: Calories 310, Carbs 7.1g, Total Fat 17.2g, Protein 29.3g

Grilled Cauliflower Steaks with Haricots Vert

Preparation time: 20 minutes

Serves: 2-4

Ingredients

- 2 tbsps. olive oil
- 1 head cauliflower, sliced lengthwise into 'steaks'
- 2 tbsps. chili sauce
- 1 tsp hot paprika
- 1 tsp oregano
- Salt and black pepper to taste
- 1 shallot, chopped
- 1 bunch haricots vert, trimmed
- 1 tbsp. fresh lemon juice
- 1 tbsp. cilantro, chopped

Directions

1. Preheat grill to medium heat. Steam the haricots vert in salted water over medium heat for 6 minutes.

2. Drain, remove to a bowl and toss with lemon juice.

3. In a bowl, mix the olive oil, chili sauce, hot paprika, and oregano. Brush the cauliflower steaks with the mixture.

4. Place them on the grill, close the lid and grill for 6 minutes. Flip the cauliflower and cook further for 6 minutes.

5. Remove the grilled caulis to a plate; sprinkle with salt, black pepper, shallots and cilantro.

6. Serve with the steamed haricots vert.

Nutritional Information: Calories 234, Carbs 8.4g, Total Fat 15.9, Protein 5.2g

Scrambled Tofu

Preparation time: 20 minutes

Serves: 2-4

Ingredients

- 7 oz. (200 g) tofu
- 4 eggs
- 1 tomato
- 1 onion
- Oil
- Curry powder
- Salt and pepper to season

Directions

1. Use a fork to crush the tofu in a bowl. Add the eggs and blend.

2. Season with curry powder and with salt and pepper and set aside for a little while. Chop the onion and the tomatoes and keep in separate bowls.

3. Heat a little oil in a pan and first lightly braise the onions until they start to brown. Then add the chopped tomatoes and sauté for 2 minutes.

4. Add the egg-tofu mixture and continue cooking until all of the egg is firm. Then taste the scrambled eggs again and if necessary season.

5. Serve the scrambled tofu on plates and enjoy warm.

Nutritional Information: Calories 162, Carbs 5,5g, Total Fat 9g, Protein 12.5g

Easy Zoodles with Sauce and Parmesan

Preparation time: 20 minutes

Serves: 2-4

Ingredients

- 1/2 avocado, pitted and peeled
- 2 tablespoons sunflower seeds, hulled
- 1 ripe tomato, quartered
- 2 tablespoons water
- Sea salt and ground black pepper, to taste
- 1/4 teaspoon dried dill weed
- 1 medium-sized zucchini, sliced
- 2 tablespoons parmesan cheese, preferably freshly grated

Directions

1. In your blender or food processor, puree the avocado, sunflower seeds, tomato, water, salt, black pepper, and dill until creamy and uniform.

2. Prepare your zoodles using a spiralizer.

3. Top the zoodles with the sauce; serve garnished with parmesan cheese.

Nutritional Information: Calories 164, Carbs 8.7g, Total Fat 13.3g, Protein 5.5g

Keto Tortilla Wraps with Vegetables

Preparation time: 10 minutes

Serves: 2-4

Ingredients

- 2 tsp olive oil
- 2 low carb tortillas
- 1 green onion, sliced
- 1 bell pepper, sliced
- ¼ tsp hot chilli powder
- 1 large avocado, sliced
- 1 cup cauli rice
- Salt and black pepper to taste
- ¼ cup sour cream
- 1 tbsp. Mexican salsa
- 1 tbsp. cilantro, chopped

Directions

1. Warm the olive oil in a skillet and sauté the green onion and bell pepper until they start to brown on the edges, for about 4 minutes; remove to a bowl.

2. To the same pan, add in the cauli rice and stir-fry for 4-5 minutes.

3. Combine with the onion and bell pepper mixture, season with salt, black pepper, and chili powder. Let cool for a few minutes.

4. Add in avocado, sour cream, and Mexican salsa and stir. Top with cilantro.

5. Fold in the sides of each tortilla, and roll them in and over the filling to be enclosed.

6. Wrap with foil, cut in halves, and serve.

Nutritional Information: Calories 373, Carbs 8.6g, Total Fat 31.2g, Protein 7.6g

Avocado-Mint Smoothie

Preparation time: 10 minutes

Serves: 2-4

Ingredients

- 1 1/2 c (400 g) Greek yogurt
- 1/2 lb. (200 g) avocado
- 10 mint leaves

Directions

1. Peel the avocados, removing all woody areas with a sharp knife.

2. Chop the flesh and add into a shaker.

3. Add the yogurt and blend into a creamy smoothie on high. Add the mint leaves and blend another 30 seconds.

4. Pour the smoothie into cups and serve promptly. Or refrigerate and enjoy later.

Nutritional Information: Calories 210, Carbs 8.5g, Total Fat 17g, Protein 4.3g

Fruit Salad with Yogurt-Basil Dressing

Preparation time: 20 minutes

Serves: 2-4

Ingredients

- 3/4 c (200 g) Greek yogurt
- 1/2 lb. (200 g) strawberries
- 2/3 c (100 g) blackberries
- 1 papaya
- 15 basil leaves
- 1 Tbs balsamic vinegar
- Pepper to season

Directions

1. Cut the strawberries in half, cut the papaya into cubes and add both of these and the blackberries to a bowl. Toss with salad servers.

2. Finely chop the basil and mix with the yogurt and balsamic vinegar. I desired, season to taste with pepper. This goes just as well with fruit as balsamic vinegar.

3. Pour the dressing over the fruit salad.

4. Serve promptly or infuse in the fridge.

Nutritional Information: Calories 90, Carbs 2.5g, Total Fat 5.1g, Protein 5.1g

Mediterranean Eggplant Squash Pasta

Preparation time: 15 minutes

Serves: 2

Ingredients

- 2 tbsps. butter
- 1 cup cherry tomatoes
- 2 tbsps. parsley, chopped
- 1 eggplant, cubed
- ¼ cup Parmesan cheese
- 3 tbsps. scallions, chopped
- 1 cup green beans
- 1 tsp lemon zest
- 10 oz. butternut squash, spirals

Directions

1. In a saucepan over medium heat, add the butter to melt.

2. Cook the spaghetti squash for 4-5 minutes and remove to a plate. In the same saucepan, cook eggplant for 5 minutes until tender.

3. Add the tomatoes and green beans, and cook for 5 more minutes.

4. Stir in parsley, zest, and scallions, and remove the pan from heat.

5. Stir in spaghetti squash and Parmesan cheese to serve.

Nutritional Information: Calories 388, Carbs 9.6g, Total Fat 17.8g, Protein 12g

Bell Pepper Omelet

Preparation time: 20 minutes

Serves: 2-4

Ingredients

- 6 eggs
- 4 marinated bell peppers
- 1 garlic clove
- Olive oil
- Salt and pepper to season

Directions

1. Dice the marinated bell pepper and mince the garlic.

2. Beat the eggs in a bowl and mix with the bell pepper and garlic. Season with salt and pepper. Heat a non-stick pan with a little oil.

3. Coat the bottom of the pan with the egg mixture. Cook until the sides start to set.

4. Turn the omelet and also cook the other side until golden brown. Repeat with the remaining omelets. Then fold the omelets in half and serve promptly.

Nutritional Information: Calories 295, Carbs 2.6g, Total Fat 7.4g, Protein 9g

Apple-Walnut Granola

Preparation time: 20 minutes

Serves: 2-4

Ingredients

- 2 apples
- 1 c (100 g) sliced almonds
- 1/2 c (50 g) chopped walnuts
- 7 Tbs (100 ml) milk
- Cinnamon

Directions

1. Peel the apples and cut into small pieces or sticks. Add into a bowl.
2. Mix with the sliced almonds and chopped walnuts.
3. Season the granola with a pinch of cinnamon.
4. Add the milk and serve promptly.

Nutritional Information: Calories 296, Carbs 12.2g, Total Fat 22.8g, Protein 8g

Broccoli Slaw with Tahini Dressing

Preparation time: 10 minutes

Serves: 2

Ingredients

Salad

- 1/2 cup broccoli florets
- 1 bell pepper, seeded and sliced
- 1 shallot, thinly sliced
- 1/2 cup arugula
- 2 ounces mozzarella cheese
- 2 tablespoons toasted sunflower seeds

Tahini Dressing

- 1 tablespoon freshly squeezed lemon juice
- 1/4 cup tahini (sesame butter)
- 1 garlic clove, minced
- 1/2 teaspoon yellow mustard
- 1/2 teaspoon ground black pepper
- Pink salt, to taste

Directions

Place the cabbage, pepper, shallot, and arugula in a nice salad bowl. Mix all ingredients for the dressing. Now, dress your salad and top with the mozzarella cheese and sunflower seeds. Serve at room temperature or well chilled.

Scrambled Egg with Feta

Preparation time: 10 minutes

Serves: 2-4

Ingredients

- 6 eggs
- 1/4 lb (100 g) feta
- 6 cocktail tomatoes
- 1 onion
- Olive oil
- Salt and pepper to season

Directions

1. Cut the tomatoes in half, peel and cube the onions and keep in separate bowls.

2. Beat the eggs in a bowl and whisk. Then season the egg mixture with salt and pepper. In a pan with a little oil first sauté the onions until slightly light brown.

3. Add the eggs and cook briefly until set. Pull apart the firm eggs.

4. Lastly, add the tomato halves, tear the feta with your hands and also heat in the pan. Sauté another 2 minutes on medium, arrange on plates and serve promptly.

Nutritional Information: Calories 195, Carbs 1.6g, Total Fat 19.5g, Protein 13.1g

Roasted Cauliflower Gratin

Preparation time: 21 minutes

Serves: 2-4

Ingredients

- 1/3 cup butter
- 2 tbsps. melted butter
- 1 onion, chopped
- 2 heads cauliflower, cut into florets
- Salt and black pepper to taste
- ¼ cup almond milk
- ½ cup almond flour
- 1 ½ cups cheddar cheese, grated
- 1 tbsp. ground almonds
- 1 tbsp. parsley, chopped

Directions

1. Steam the cauliflower in salted water for 4-5 minutes. Drain and set aside.

2. Melt the 1/3 cup of butter in a saucepan over medium heat and sauté the onion for 3 minutes.

3. Add the cauliflower, season with salt and black pepper and mix in almond milk. Simmer for 3 minutes.

4. Mix the remaining melted butter with the almond flour. Stir into the cauliflower as well as half of the cheese.

5. Sprinkle the top with the remaining cheese and ground almonds, and bake for 10 minutes until golden brown on the top.

6. Serve sprinkled with parsley.

Nutritional Information: **Calories 455, Carbs 6.5g, Total Fat 38.3g, Protein 16.3g**

Easy Creamy Broccoli Soup

Preparation time: 15 minutes

Serves: 2

Ingredients

- 1 tablespoon butter, at room temperature
- 1/2 small-sized leek, chopped
- 1/4 cup celery rib, chopped
- 1/2 teaspoon ginger garlic paste
- 1 ½ cups broccoli florets
- 1 ½ cups roasted vegetable broth
- 1 bay laurel
- 1 thyme sprig, chopped
- 1 cup spinach leaves
- Kosher salt and ground black pepper, to taste
- 2 tablespoons cream cheese
- 1 tablespoon tahini butter
- 1/3 cup yogurt

Directions

1. In a Dutch pot, melt the butter over medium-high heat.
2. Now, sauté the leeks and celery until just tender and fragrant.

3. Add the ginger-garlic paste and continue cooking an additional 30 seconds or until aromatic.

4. Now, stir in the broccoli, broth, bay laurel, and thyme, and bring it to a rapid boil.

5. Then, turn the heat to low and let it simmer, covered, for a further 5 to 8 minutes.

6. After that, stir in the spinach, salt, and black pepper; let it simmer for 2 minutes more or until the leaves have wilted.

7. Transfer the soup to a food processor; add the cream cheese and tahini butter; process until everything is smooth and uniform.

8. Swirl the yogurt into the soup and serve warm.

Nutritional Information: Calories 208, Carbs 6.4g, Total Fat 15.9g, Protein 8.8g

Mediterranean Cauliflower Quiche with Cheese

Preparation time: 15 minutes

Serves: 2

Ingredients

- 1/2-pound small cauliflower florets
- 1/2 cup vegetable broth
- 2 scallions, chopped
- 1 teaspoon garlic, crushed
- 1/2 cup full-fat milk
- 2 eggs, whisked
- Sea salt and ground black pepper, to taste
- 1/2 teaspoon paprika
- 1/2 teaspoon basil
- 1/2 teaspoon oregano
- 1-ounce sour cream
- 3 ounces Provolone cheese, freshly grated

Directions

1. Cook the cauliflower with the vegetable broth over medium-low flame until tender but crispy.

2. Transfer the cauliflower florets to a lightly greased casserole dish. Then, preheat your oven to 360 degrees F.

3. In a mixing dish, thoroughly combine the scallions, garlic, milk, eggs, salt, black pepper, paprika, basil, and oregano.

4. Pour the scallion mixture over the cauliflower florets.

5. Mix the sour cream and Provolone cheese; add the cheese mixture to the top.

6. Cover with foil. Bake in the preheated oven for about 45 minutes, until topping is lightly golden and everything is heated through.

7. Transfer to a cooling rack for 10 minutes before serving.

Nutritional Information: Calories 208, Carbs 6.4g, Total Fat 15.9g, Protein 8.8g

Chili & Blue Cheese Stuffed Mushrooms

Preparation time: 30 minutes

Serves: 2

Ingredients

- 1 tbsp. olive oil
- 4 Portobello mushrooms, stems removed
- 1 cup blue cheese, crumbled
- 2 sprigs fresh thyme, chopped
- ½ chili pepper chopped
- Salt and black pepper to taste
- 2 tbsps. ground walnuts

Nutritional Information: Calories 368, Carbs 3.9g, Total Fat 31.5g, Protein 18.8g

Zucchini and Mushroom Lasagna

Preparation time: 1 hr. 20 minutes

Serves: 2-4

Ingredients

- 1 large-sized zucchini, sliced lengthwise
- 1 tablespoon olive oil
- 1 red bell pepper, chopped
- 1 shallot, chopped
- 1/2-pound chestnut mushrooms, chopped
- 2 cloves garlic, pressed
- Sea salt and ground black pepper, to season
- 1/4 teaspoon red pepper flakes
- 1/4 teaspoon dried oregano
- 1/2 teaspoon dried dill weed
- 1 vine-ripe tomato, pureed
- 1 egg, whisked
- 1/2 cup Greek-style yogurt
- 1/2 cup Provolone cheese, grated

Directions

1. Place the zucchini slices in a bowl with a colander; add 1 teaspoon of salt and let it stand for 12 to 15 minutes; gently squeeze to discard the excess water.

2. Grill the zucchini slices for 3 minutes per side until beginning to brown; reserve. Heat the olive oil in a skillet over moderate flame.

3. Now, sauté the pepper and shallot until they have softened.

4. Next, stir in the mushrooms and garlic; continue sautéing until they are just fragrant. Add in the spices and pureed tomatoes and let it cook until heated through or about 5 minutes.

5. Pour the mushroom/tomato sauce on the bottom of a lightly greased baking pan. Arrange the zucchini slices on top.

6. Mix the egg with the Greek yogurt; add the mixture to the top. Top with the grated Provolone cheese and transfer to the preheated oven.

7. Bake at 370 degrees F approximately 45 minutes until the cheese is melted and the edges are bubbling.

8. Let your lasagna stand for about 8 minutes before slicing and serving.

Nutritional Information: Calories 284, Carbs 7.9g, Total Fat 18.3g, Protein 20g

Burritos Wraps with Avocado & Cauliflower

Preparation time: 5 minutes

Serves: 2

Ingredients

- 1 tbsp. butter
- ½ head cauliflower, cut into florets
- 2 zero carb flatbread
- 1 cup yogurt
- 1 cup tomato salsa
- 1 avocado, sliced
- 1 tbsp. cilantro, chopped

Directions

1. Put the cauliflower in a food processor and pulse until it resembles rice.
2. In a skillet, melt the butter and add the cauli rice.
3. Sauté for 4-5 minutes until cooked through.
4. Season with salt and black pepper.
5. On flatbread, spread the yogurt all over and distribute the salsa on top.
6. Top with cauli rice and scatter the avocado slices and cilantro on top.
7. Fold and tuck the burritos and cut into two.

Nutritional Information: Calories 457, Carbs 9.6g, Total Fat 18.3g, Protein 15.8g

Clarion Ulreich

Parmesan Fried Eggs

Preparation time: 15 minutes

Serves: 2-4

Ingredients

- 4 eggs
- 1 1/2 oz (40 g) Parmesan
- 1 garlic clove
- Oil
- Salt and pepper to season

Directions

1. Peel and mince the garlic clove. Sauté in a pan with a little oil.

2. Break the eggs into a pan, either all at once or one at a time. Season with salt and pepper.

3. Once the eggs are firm, sprinkle with Parmesan and heat another 30 seconds on medium.

4. Arrange on plates and serve warm. If desired, season with fresh herbs.

Nutritional Information: Calories 140, Total Fats 10.2g, Carbs 1.4g, Protein 9.8g

Red Beet Salad

Preparation time: 30 minutes

Serves: 2-4

Ingredients

- 1/2 lb (200 g) fresh red beets
- 1/2 lb (200 g) radicchio
- 1 avocado
- 1 lemon
- Olive oil
- Salt and pepper to season

Directions

1. Cook the red beets in a pot on the stove for about 15 minutes. Do not peel the red beets and if desired add a little salt to the water.

2. Put the red beets on a plate and let cool a bit. Peel and slice or dice with a sharp knife. Here it's best to use disposable gloves so your hands won't stain. Red beets are also available precooked and canned. This will make preparation easier and reduce the overall cooking time.

3. Cut or pluck the radicchio into pieces, wash and dry with a salad spinner. Remove the flesh from the avocado and dice, grate the lemon zest and squeeze the lemon.

4. Add the red beets, lettuce, lemon zest and avocado to a bowl and mix well. For the dressing mix the lemon juice with olive oil, then season with salt and pepper.

5. Pour the dressing over the salad and toss with salad servers. Then serve promptly.

Nutritional Information: Calories 159, Total Fats 11g, Carbs 10.8g, Protein 2.8g

Hot Pizza with Tomatoes, Cheese & Olives

Preparation time: 30 minutes

Serves: 2-4

Ingredients

- 2 tbsps. psyllium husk
- 1 cup cheddar cheese
- 2 tbsps. cream cheese
- 2 tbsps. Pecorino cheese
- 1 tsp oregano
- ½ cup almond flour

Topping

- 1 tomato, sliced
- 4 oz. cheddar cheese, sliced
- ¼ cup tomato sauce
- 1 jalapeño pepper, sliced
- ½ cup black olives
- 2 tbsps. basil, chopped

Directions

1. Preheat the oven to 375 F. Microwave the cheddar cheese in an oven-proof bowl. In a separate bowl, combine cream cheese, pecorino cheese, psyllium husk, almond flour, and oregano.

2. Add in the melted cheddar cheese and mix with your hands to combine.

3. Divide the dough in two. Roll out the two crusts in circles and place on a lined baking sheet. Bake for about 10 minutes.

4. Spread the tomato sauce over the crust and top with the cheddar cheese slices, jalapeño pepper, and tomato slices. Return to the oven and bake for another 10 minutes.

5. Garnish with black olives and basil.

Nutritional Information: Calories 576, Total Fats 42.6g, Carbs 7.5g, Protein 32.4g

Grilled Tofu Kabobs with Arugula Salad

Preparation time: 40 minutes + Marinade time

Serves: 2-4

Ingredients

- 14 oz. firm tofu, cut into strips
- 4 tsp sesame oil
- 1 lemon, juiced
- 5 tbsps. soy sauce, sugar-free
- 3 tsp garlic powder
- 4 tbsps. coconut flour
- ½ cup sesame seeds

Arugula salad

- 4 cups arugula, chopped
- 2 tsp extra virgin olive oil
- 2 tbsps. pine nuts
- Salt and black pepper to season
- 1 tbsp. balsamic vinegar

Directions

1. Stick the tofu strips on the skewers, height-wise and place onto a plate.

2. In a bowl, mix sesame oil, lemon juice, soy sauce, garlic powder, and coconut flour.

3. Pour the soy sauce mixture over the tofu, and turn in the sauce to be adequately coated.

4. Cover the dish with cling film and marinate in the fridge for 2 hours.

5. Heat the griddle pan over high heat. Coat the tofu in the sesame seeds and grill in the griddle pan to be golden brown on both sides, about 12 minutes in total.

6. Arrange the arugula on a serving plate.

7. Drizzle over olive oil and balsamic vinegar, and season with salt and black pepper.

8. Sprinkle with pine nuts and place the tofu kabobs on top to serve.

Nutritional Information: Calories 411, Total Fats 32.9g, Carbs 7.1g, Protein 21.6g

Cream of Tomato Soup

Preparation time: 30 minutes

Serves: 2-4

Ingredients

- 1 large can of tomatoes
- 1 2/3 c (400 ml) vegetable broth
- 1 c (250 g) yogurt
- 1 oz. (30 g) ginger
- 1 Spanish onion
- Oil
- Salt and pepper to season

Directions

1. Peel and dice the Spanish onion and ginger. Lightly braise in a pot with a little oil until translucent. Then add the can of tomatoes.

2. Add the vegetable broth. Bring to a boil, then simmer on medium for 15 minutes. Briefly remove the pot from the burner and puree with an immersion blender. If the tomato soup is too thin, you can add some tomato paste to thicken it up.

3. Reheat the soup and stir in the yogurt a little at a time. Season to taste with salt and pepper and serve on plates or in a tureen. If desired, garnish with fresh herbs, e.g. basil.

Nutritional Information: Calories 125, Total Fats 9g, Carbs 6.7g, Protein 3.2g

*The Complete
Keto For Two Beginners Cookbook*

Green Omelet

Preparation time: 20 minutes

Serves: 2-4

Ingredients

- 1/4 lb. (100 g) spinach
- 4 eggs
- 2 green onions
- Oil
- Salt and pepper to season

Directions

1. Thinly slice the green onions, add into a bowl and set aside for a little while. Then remove the wilted spinach leaves, wash the rest of the spinach and dry in a salad spinner.

2. In a separate bowl beat the eggs with salt and pepper. Then add the eggs and the spinach to a blender and blend on high for about 1 minute.

3. Heat a pan with oil on the stove and first lightly braise the green onions in it. Once they have taken a little color add the egg and spinach mixture. Flip when the edges of the omelet are firm. The remaining cooking time is about half as long as the first side.

4. Arrange on a plate and fold in half before serving. This dish is perfect for invitations, since you can easily make the salmon-cream cheese spread for non-vegetarian guests, which goes perfectly with the spinach flavor.

Nutritional Information: Calories 404, Total Fats 7.4g, Carbs 6.5g, Protein 2.1g

The Complete
Keto For Two Beginners Cookbook

Zucchini Pasta with Caper Pesto

Preparation time: 25 minutes

Serves: 2-4

Ingredients

- 2 zucchini
- 1 garlic clove
- 2 oz. (50 g) arugula
- 2 oz. (50 g) Parmesan
- 2 Tbs (20 g) capers
- Oil
- Salt and pepper to season

Directions

1. First prepare the pesto. Peel and mince the garlic clove. Add arugula, capers, Parmesan and a little oil to a shaker to make a creamy pesto.

2. Start with just a little oil and add more if necessary. If desired, season the pesto with salt and pepper to taste and refrigerate to infuse until ready to serve.

3. Next wash the zucchini and peel with a vegetable peeler. The shape of the vegetable pasta should be similar to fettuccine.

4. Heat a pan with oil on the stove and lightly braise the zucchini strips for about 3-4 minutes.

5. Divide the zucchini pasta on plates and garnish with dollops of pesto.

Nutritional Information: Calories 95, Total Fats 6.5g, Carbs 2.9g, Protein 6.3g

Zucchini Carpaccio

Preparation time: 20 minutes

Serves: 2-4

Ingredients

- 2 zucchini
- 1 red onion
- 1 Tbs mustard
- Sherry vinegar
- Oil
- Salt and pepper to season

Directions

1. To prepare the zucchini, first wash, then thinly slice.

2. Season with salt and pepper in a bowl and toss well.

3. Heat a pan with oil on the stove and sauté the seasoned zucchini slices golden brown from both sides. Arrange the zucchini on plates or a platter. To make the dressing, first dice the red onion.

4. In a small bowl mix equal parts of sherry vinegar and oil. Stir in 1 tsp mustard and the diced onion.

5. Season to taste with salt and pepper, drizzle the dressing over the zucchini carpaccio, then if possible serve warm.

Nutritional Information: Calories 90, Total Fats 8g, Carbs 2.1g, Protein 4.2g

Scalloped Fennel

Preparation time: 30 minutes

Serves: 2-4

Ingredients

- 4 bulbs of fennel
- 3 1/2 c (750 ml) vegetable broth
- 5 oz. (150 g) mozzarella
- Olive oil
- Salt and pepper to season

Directions

1. To prepare the bulbs of fennel, remove the stalk and leaves.

2. Cook the remaining bulb in hot water with salt or vegetable broth for about 10 minutes. Then cut the fennel in half and add into a casserole dish. Season with salt and pepper.

3. Add a little of the vegetable broth and top the halves with the sliced mozzarella.

4. Bake in a preheated oven at 400°F (200°C) for 10-15 minutes. Once the mozzarella is golden brown the food is done. Serve warm.

Nutritional Information: Calories 200, Total Fats 13.1g, Carbs 6.6g, Protein 12.6g

Pizza Bianca with Mushrooms

Preparation time: 30 minutes

Serves: 2-4

Ingredients

- 2 tbsps. olive oil
- 4 eggs
- 2 tbsps. water
- 1 jalapeño pepper, diced
- ¼ cup mozzarella cheese, shredded
- 2 chives, chopped
- 2 cups egg Alfredo sauce
- ½ tsp oregano
- ½ cup mushrooms, sliced

Directions

1. Preheat oven to 360 F. In a bowl, whisk eggs, water, and oregano.
2. Heat the olive oil in a large skillet.
3. Pour in the egg mixture and cook until set, flipping once.
4. Remove and spread the alfredo sauce and jalapeño pepper all over.
5. Top with mozzarella cheese, mushrooms and chives.
6. Bake for 5-10 minutes until the cheese melts.

Nutritional Information: Calories 312, Total Fats 23.5g, Carbs 2.4g, Protein 17.2g

Made in the USA
Las Vegas, NV
16 January 2025

16464242R10194